Global Civil Society

Global Civil Society

An Answer to War

MARY KALDOR

polity

First published in 2003 by Polity Press in association with Blackwell Publishing Ltd

Editorial office:
Polity Press
65 Bridge Street
Cambridge CB2 1UR, UK

Marketing and production:
Blackwell Publishing Ltd
108 Cowley Road
Oxford OX4 1JF, UK

Distributed in the USA by
Blackwell Publishing Inc.
350 Main Street
Malden, MA 02148, USA

A catalogue record for this book is available from the British Library.

Library of Congress Cataloging-in-Publication Data

Kaldor, Mary.
Global civil society : an answer to war / Mary Kaldor.
     p. cm.
Includes bibliographical references and index.
ISBN 0-7456-2757-9 – ISBN 0-7456-2758-7 (pbk.)
1. Civil society. 2. Globalization. I. Title.
JC337 .K35 2003
300–dc21
2002014306

Typeset 11 on 13 pt Berling
by Kolam Information Services Pvt. Ldt. Pondicherry, India.
Printed and bound in Great Britain by MPG Books Ltd, Bodmin, Cornwall

For further information on Polity, visit our website: www.polity.co.uk

Contents

Preface

In a lecture at the London School of Economics in October 1999, Adam Michnik pointed out that everyone claims responsibility for the end of the Cold War:

> Whenever I happen to consider that topic – why Communism failed – I know that in Washington, everybody is sure that Communism failed as a result of the American policy – how else?... Whenever I am in the Vatican, it seems perfectly clear that Communism fell as a result of the activities of the Apostolic See and John Paul II, our pope.... Whenever I am in Asia, I have no doubts that Communism was lost in Afghanistan. That it was just there where the Soviet Union broke its teeth. And whenever I am in Moscow, it is absolutely obvious to me that Communism was toppled by Russians, the only thing that remains unclear being whether it was by Gorbachev or Yeltsin. And finally, we Poles know and are convinced that it was we who toppled Communism and that the world received freedom from Communism from us, as a gift.

This book has its starting point in the debates and dialogue between the West European peace movement and the East European opposition in the 1980s, in which I was deeply engaged and which has left a lasting imprint on my political understanding. While we in the peace movement did not think that we were responsible for the fall of communism we did feel that we had played a part and that, in the subsequent triumph of neoliberalism, our part was written out of history. The ideas that we developed at that time and the efforts we made to influence the behaviour of governments and international institutions were *both* about democratization and human rights *and* about peace and international security. Indeed, we believed that these issues were deeply interconnected since the organization of states for war constituted a profound limitation on democracy. The idea of a 'transcontinental movement of citizens', in the words of E. P. Thompson, was the genesis of the notion of global civil society.

Subsequently, I and others tried to put these ideas into practice in the Helsinki Citizens Assembly – a network of groups and individuals, whose aim was to create a pan-European civil society. We found ourselves confronting a very different world. If the Cold War of 1945–89 was actually experienced as a kind of peace, albeit an oppressive peace, then the Orwellian post-Cold War peace is actually experienced as war, not only in the Balkans or Africa but in the urban ghettos of the new global cities. We found that global civil society did not only include human rights and peace groups like us but also new nationalist and fundamentalist groups and, as the 1990s drew to a close, a new radical anti-capitalist movement as well.

Since 1999, I have been able to spend time reading and thinking about these issues and discussing ideas with my colleagues in the Global Civil Society programme. Thus this book is the product both of activism and analysis and I should like to thank all those, who are too numerous to mention, who were involved in the dialogue of the 1980s, the Helsinki Citizens Assembly in the 1990s as well as my colleagues both at Sussex and LSE, from whom I have learned such a lot.

I am especially grateful to David Held, who proposed and promoted the project, to Meghnad Desai, who read the manuscript twice and was always ready to stop everything to help think an argument through, and to Jo Hay for moral and administrative support. I am also grateful to all those who read and commented on all or parts of the manuscript and who discussed the ideas with me, including Nancy Cartwright, Mient Jan Faber, Marlies Glasius, Julian Robinson and Yahia Said. Finally, I want to thank everyone at Polity, including the anonymous readers, who were all unfailingly helpful.

Chapter 3 is based on a lecture I gave at the London School of Economics in October 1999 in a series called 'The Ideas of 1989'.

Earlier versions have been published in *Transnational Law and Contemporary Problems*, vol. 9, no. 2 (Fall 1999); and in R. Falk, L. E. J. Ruiz and R. B. J. Walker (eds), *Reframing the International: Law, Culture, Politics* (Routledge, 2002).

Abbreviations

ATTAC	Action pour une Taxe Tobin d'Aide aux Citoyens
BJP	Bharatiya Janata Party
CARE	Cooperative for American Relief Everywhere
CBO	community building organization
CSCE	Conference on Security and Cooperation in Europe
DRC	Democratic Republic of Congo
END	European Nuclear Disarmament
FIDESZ	Young Democrats, now Hungarian Civic Party
GRO	grass roots organization
ICC	International Criminal Court
ICRC	International Committee of the Red Cross
ICT	information and communications technology
IMF	International Monetary Fund
INF	intermediate nuclear weapons
INGO	international non-governmental organization
KLA	Kosovo Liberation Army
MSF	Médecins sans Frontières
Nato	North Atlantic Treaty Organization
NGO	non-governmental organization
NMD	national missile defense
OECD	Organization for Economic Cooperation and Development
UNICEF	United Nations Children's Fund

1
Five Meanings of Global Civil Society

The terms 'global' and 'civil society' became the new buzzwords of the 1990s. In this book, I want to suggest that the two terms are interconnected and reflect a new reality, however imperfectly understood. The reinvention of 'civil society' in the 1970s and 1980s, simultaneously in Latin America and Eastern Europe, had something to do with the global context – the social, political and economic transformations that were taking place in different parts of the world and that came to the surface after 1989. Indeed, although the term 'civil society' has a long history and its contemporary meanings draw on that history, the various ways in which it is used, I shall argue, are quite different from in the past.

What is new about the concept of civil society since 1989 is globalization. Civil society is no longer confined to the borders of the territorial state. There was always a common core of meaning in the civil society literature, which still has relevance. Civil society was associated with a rule-governed society based largely on the consent of individual citizens rather than coercion. Different definitions of civil society have reflected the different ways in which consent was generated, manufactured, nurtured or purchased, the different rights and obligations that formed the basis of consent, and the different interpretations of this process. However, the fact that civil society was territorially bound meant that it was always contrasted with coercive rule-governed societies and with societies that lacked rules. In particular, as I shall argue, civil

society within the territorial boundaries of the state was circumscribed by war.

This is what has changed. The end of the Cold War and
growing global interconnectedness have undermined the territorial distinction between 'civil' and 'uncivil' societies, between
the 'democratic' West and the 'non-democratic' East and South,
and have called into question the traditional centralized war-
making state. And these developments, in turn, have opened
up new possibilities for political emancipation as well as new
risks and greater insecurity. Whether we are talking about
isolated dissidents in repressive regimes, landless labourers in
Central America or Asia, global campaigns against land mines or
third world debt, or even religious fundamentalists and fanatic
nationalists, what has changed are the opportunities for linking
up with other like-minded groups in different parts of the
world, and for addressing demands not just to the state but to
global institutions and other states. On the one hand, global
civil society is in the process of helping to constitute and being
constituted by a global system of rules, underpinned by overlapping inter-governmental, governmental and global authorities.
In other words, a new form of politics, which we call civil society,
is both an outcome and an agent of global interconnectedness.
And on the other hand, new forms of violence, which restrict,
suppress and assault civil society, also spill over borders so that
it is no longer possible to contain war or lawlessness territorially.

In the aftermath of the revolutions of 1989, the term 'civil
society' was taken up in widely different circles and circumstances. Yet there is no agreed definition of the term. Indeed,
its ambiguity is one of its attractions. The fact that neoliberals,
Islamicists, or post-Marxists use the same language provides
a common platform through which ideas, projects and policy
proposals can be worked out. The debate about its meaning is
part of what it is about. As John Keane suggests, the global spread
of the term and the discussion about what it betokens is, in itself,
a signal of an emerging global civil society.[1]

This global discussion has involved the resurrection of a body of
civil society literature. The search for classic texts has provided
what might be called a legitimizing narrative, which has had the
advantage of conferring respectability on the term but has also
often weakened our understanding of the novel aspects of the

rediscovery of the term. By clothing the concept in historical garb, it is possible that the past has imposed a kind of straitjacket which obscures or even confines the more radical contemporary implications. Comaroff and Comaroff talk about the 'archaeology' of civil society 'usually told, layer upon layer, as a chronological epic of ideas and authors' starting with an 'origin story' in the late 1700s. They argue that the term has become a 'neo-modern myth: consider the extent to which a diverse body of works – some of them analytic, some pragmatic and prescriptive, some purely philosophical – have begun to tell about the genesis and genealogy of the concept, even as they argue over its interpretation, its telos, its theoretical and socio-moral virtues'.[2]

The 'neo-modern myth' does obscure the implications of the break with territorially bound civil society. On the other hand, agreement about the history of the concept is part of what provides a common basis for a global conversation. The civil society literature is so diverse that it allows for selectivity; the choice of texts to be studied can be used to justify one interpretation rather than another. While the debate about earlier literature can reify particular meanings that are no longer applicable, it can also serve as a way of investigating the idea, exploring the answers to questions which were faced in earlier periods as well as today, finding out what questions were different and how they were distinguished from the present situation.

This is a book then about a political idea. It is an idea that expresses a real phenomenon, even if the boundaries of the phenomenon vary according to different definitions, and even if the shape and direction of the phenomenon are constantly changing. The investigation of these different definitions, the study of past debates as well as the actions and arguments of the present, are a way of directly influencing the phenomenon, of contributing to a changing reality, if possible for the better.

This book is subtitled an 'answer to war'. This is because the concept of civil society has always been linked to the notion of minimizing violence in social relations, to the public use of reason as a way of managing human affairs in place of submission based on fear and insecurity, or ideology and superstition. The word 'answer' does not imply that global civil society is some sort of magic formula – a solution or alternative to war. Rather it is a way of addressing the problem of war, of debating, arguing about, discussing and pressing for possible solutions or alternatives.

I will start by briefly recapitulating the context in which the term was 'reinvented'. I will then set out five different meanings of global civil society, two historical and three contemporary. And in the last section, I will outline my plan for the book, how I will investigate these different meanings and their implications for our understanding of the changing political world.

Context

Developments variously known as globalization, post-industrialism and information society came to the surface in the aftermath of the end of the Cold War. Two aspects of these developments are of particular significance in providing a context for the evolution of the concept of global civil society.

First of all, concern about personal autonomy, self-organization, private space became salient not only in Eastern Europe as a way of getting around the totalitarian militaristic state but also in other parts of the world where the paternalism and rigidity of the state in the post-war period was called into question. In the United States and Western Europe, these concerns had already surfaced in the 1960s and 1970s, with the emergence of movements concerned about civil rights, feminism or the environment. Giddens and Beck emphasize the growing importance of these concerns in societies which are increasingly complex, vulnerable to manufactured risk, and where expert systems no longer hold unquestioned sway.[3] The rediscovery of the term 'civil society' in Eastern Europe in the 1980s, therefore, had a resonance in other parts of the world. The term 'civil society' and related terms such as 'anti-politics' or 'power of the powerless' seemed to offer a discourse within which to frame parallel concerns about the ability to control the circumstances in which individuals live, about substantive empowerment of citizens. Indeed, East European thinkers like Václav Havel believed their ideas were not only applicable to Eastern Europe; they were a response to what Havel called the 'global technological civilization'.[4] While Western elites seized upon the language as evidence for the victory of actually existing democracies, the inheritors of the so-called new social movements began to use the term to express a demand for a radical extension of democracy for political as well as economic emancipation.[5]

Even though these ideas had echoes of the eighteenth-century preoccupation with restraints on state power, it seems to me that they were responses to an entirely novel situation. It was a situation characterized by the actual experience of an overbearing state, which reached into everyday life far more widely than ever before. In the case of Eastern Europe, it was experience of arbitrary power and the extension of state activity into every sphere of social life, even, at least during the Stalinist period, private life. Elsewhere, it was both the extension of state power and the rigidity and lack of responsiveness to social, economic and cultural change. As I shall argue, the character of the state has to be understood in terms of the heritage of war and Cold War. It was also a time of social, economic, technological and cultural transformations in life styles, ranging from work (greater insecurity, greater flexibility and greater inequality) to gender and family relations, which called into question institutional loyalties and assumptions about collective or traditional behaviour.

Secondly, growing interconnectedness and the end of the last great global inter-state conflict have eroded the boundaries of civil society. It was growing interconnectedness that allowed the emergence of 'islands of civic engagement' in Eastern Europe and in those Latin American countries suffering from military dictatorships. The activists of that period were able to seek international allies both at governmental and non-governmental levels and pierce through the closed societies in which they lived, even before the great advances in information and communications technology. On the one hand, the extension of transnational legal arrangements from above, for example the Helsinki Agreement of 1975, provided an instrument for opening up autonomous spaces in Eastern Europe and elsewhere. On the other hand, the inheritors of the 'new' social movements, the European peace movements and the North American human rights movements were able to link up with groups and individuals in Eastern Europe and Latin America to provide some kind of support and protection. Keck and Sikkink use the term the 'boomerang effect' to describe the way civil society groups bypassed the state and appealed to transnational networks and institutions as well as foreign governments, so that their demands bounced back, as it were, on their own situation.[6] In effect, these movements and their successors made use of and contributed to global political and legal arrangements; they were an essential part of the process of constructing a framework for global governance.

The end of the Cold War has contributed to the breakdown of the sharp distinction between internal and external, what is often called in the International Relations literature the Great Divide.[7] Some argue that something like a global civil society (however this is defined) exists in the North Atlantic region but not elsewhere.[8] Hence the boundaries of civil society have merely moved outwards. This could perhaps have been said to be true during the Cold War where the boundaries of the West were pushed outwards to protect a North Atlantic group of nations. But, in the aftermath of the Cold War, I would suggest that something different is happening. It is no longer possible to insulate territory from anarchy and disorder. In place of vertical territorial-based forms of civil society, we are witnessing the emergence of horizontal transnational global networks, both civil and uncivil. What one might call zones of civility and zones of incivility exist side by side in the same territorial space; North Atlantic space may have more extensive zones of civility than other parts of the world but such sharp geographic distinctions can no longer be drawn. The events of September 11 were a traumatic expression of the fact that territorial borders no longer define the zones of civility. In other words, the territorial restructuring of social, economic and political relations has profound implications for how we think about civil society.[9]

To sum up, I want to suggest that the discussion about global civil society has to be understood in terms of what one might call deepening and widening, a move away from state-centred approaches, combining more concern with individual empowerment and person autonomy, as well as a territorial restructuring of social and political relations in different realms.

Definitions of global civil society

I propose to set out five different versions of the concept of civil society in common usage and to say something about what they imply in a global context. This is a non-exhaustive and abbreviated (but not altogether arbitrary) list. As I try to show in chapter 2, the civil society literature is much richer and more complex than this summary would suggest; the aim is to set up some parameters for the rest of the book.

The first two versions are drawn from past versions of the concept; the last three are contemporary versions, with echoes of historical usage. It is not straightforward to transpose the concept of civil society into the concept of global civil society, since, as I have argued, the key to understanding what is new about contemporary meanings is precisely their global character. Yet the exercise may be illuminating since I do believe that there is a common core of meaning and we can investigate the nature of the contemporary phenomenon by trying to understand the relevance of past meanings.

Societas civilis

Here I am referring to what could be described as the original version of the term – civil society as a rule of law and a political community, a peaceful order based on implicit or explicit consent of individuals, a zone of 'civility'. Civility is defined not just as 'good manners' or 'polite society' but as a state of affairs where violence has been minimized as a way of organizing social relations. It is public security that creates the basis for more 'civil' procedures for settling conflicts – legal arrangements, for example, or public deliberation. Most later definitions of civil society are predicated on the assumption of a rule of law and the relative absence of coercion in human affairs at least within the boundaries of the state. Thus, it is assumed that such a *societas civilis* requires a state, with a public monopoly of legitimate violence. According to this definition, the meaning of civil society cannot be separated from the existence of a state. Civil society is distinguished not from the state but from non-civil societies – the state of nature or absolutist empires – and from war.

One of the main objections to the notion of global civil society is the absence of a world state.[10] However, it can be argued that the coming together of humanitarian and human rights law, the establishment of an international criminal court, the expansion of international peacekeeping, betoken an emerging framework of global governance, what Immanuel Kant described as a universal civil society, in the sense of a cosmopolitan rule of law, guaranteed by a combination of international treaties and institutions.

Bourgeois society (*Bürgerliche Gesellschaft*)

For Hegel and Marx, civil society was that arena of ethical life in between the state and the family. It was a historically produced phenomenon linked to the emergence of capitalism. They drew on the insights of the Scottish enlightenment, especially Adam Smith and Adam Ferguson, who argued that the advent of commercial society created the individuals who were the necessary condition for civil society. Markets, social classes, civil law and welfare organizations were all part of civil society. Civil society was, for the first time, contrasted with the state. For Hegel, civil society was the 'achievement of the modern age'. And for Marx, civil society was the 'theatre of history'.[11]

Transposed to a global level, civil society could be more or less equated with 'globalization from below' – all those aspects of global developments below and beyond the state and international political institutions, including transnational corporations, foreign investment, migration, global culture, etc.[12]

The activist version

The activist perspective is probably closest to the version of civil society that emerged from the opposition in Central Europe in the 1970s and 1980s. It is sometimes described as the post-Marxist or utopian version of the concept. It is a definition that presupposes a state or rule of law, but insists not only on restraints on state power but on a redistribution of power. It is a radicalization of democracy and an extension of participation and autonomy. On this definition, civil society refers to active citizenship, to growing self-organization outside formal political circles, and expanded space in which individual citizens can influence the conditions in which they live both directly through self-organization and through political pressure.

What is important, according to this definition, at a transnational level is the existence of a global public sphere – a global space where non-instrumental communication can take place, inhabited by transnational advocacy networks like Greenpeace or Amnesty International, global social movements like the protestors in Seattle, Prague and Genoa, international media through which their campaigns can be brought to global attention, new global 'civic religions' like human rights or environmentalism.

The neoliberal version

In the aftermath of 1989, neoliberals claimed their victory and began to popularize the term 'civil society' as what the West has, or even what the United States has. This version might be described as 'laissez-faire politics', a kind of market in politics. According to this definition, civil society consists of associational life – a non-profit, voluntary 'third sector' – that not only restrains state power but also actually provides a substitute for many of the functions performed by the state. Thus charities and voluntary associations carry out functions in the field of welfare which the state can no longer afford to perform. This definition is perhaps the easiest to transpose to the global arena; it is viewed as the political or social counterpart of the process of globalization understood as economic globalization, liberalization, privatization, deregulation and the growing mobility of capital and goods. In the absence of a global state, an army of NGOs (non-governmental organizations) perform the functions necessary to smooth the path of economic globalization. Humanitarian NGOs provide the safety net to deal with the casualties of liberalization and privatization strategies in the economic field. Funding for democracy-building and human rights NGOs is somehow supposed to help establish a rule of law and respect for human rights. Thus critics have charged that the term is reactionary, a way of evading the responsibilities of states for welfare or security.[13]

The postmodern version

The postmodern definition of civil society departs from the universalism of the activist and neoliberal versions, although even this version requires one universal principle – that of tolerance.[14] Civil society is an arena of pluralism and contestation, a source of incivility as well as civility. Some postmodernists criticize the concept of civil society as Eurocentric; a product of a specific Western culture that is imposed on the rest of the world. Others suggest a reformulation so as to encompass other more communalist understandings of political culture. In particular, it is argued that classic Islamic society represented a form of civil society in the balance between religion, the bazaar and the ruler.

For the activist version, the inhabitants of civil society can be roughly equated with civic-minded or public-spirited groups. Those active in civil society would be those concerned about public affairs and public debate. For the postmodernists, civic-minded groups are only one component of civil society. In particular, postmodernists emphasize the importance of national and religious identities as well as multiple identities as a precondition for civil society, whereas for the activists, a shared cosmopolitanism is more important. Whether or not groups advocating violence should be included is open to question.

From this perspective, it is possible to talk about global civil society in the sense of the global spread of fields of contestation. Indeed, one might talk about a plurality of global civil societies through different globally organized networks. These might include Islam, nationalist Diaspora networks, as well as human rights networks etc.

These five versions are summarized in table 1.1. My own understanding of global civil society, which I shall explore in this book, incorporates much of these different meanings. I do believe that both the first two versions, a rule of law and a market society, or at least the aspiration for a rule of law and for economic autonomy, are constituted and constituted by what we now tend

Table 1.1   The five versions of civil society

Type of society	Territorially bounded	Global
Societas civilis	Rule of law/Civility	Cosmopolitan order
Bürgerliche Gesellschaft	All organized social life between the state and the family	Economic, social and cultural globalization
Activist	Social movements, civic activists	A global public sphere
Neoliberal	Charities, voluntary associations, third sector	Privatization of democracy building, humanitarianism
Postmodern	Nationalists, fundamentalists as well as above	Plurality of global networks of contestation

to mean by civil society; for civil society to exist there has to be a relationship with markets, which secure economic autonomy, and the rule of law, which provides security. I also think that the various actors that inhabit contemporary versions of civil society are all part of global civil society – the social movements and the civic networks of the activist version; the charities, voluntary associations and what I shall call the 'tamed' NGOs of the neo-liberal version; and the nationalist and fundamentalist groups that are included in the postmodern version.

In terms of normative considerations, however, I am closest to the activist version. All versions of civil society are both norma tive and descriptive. They describe a political project i.e. a goal, and at the same time an actually existing reality, which may not measure up to the goal. *Societas civilis* expressed the goal of public security, of a civilized, i.e. non-violent, society. *Bürgerliche Gesellschaft* was about the rise of market society as a condition for individual freedom, and the balance between the state and the market. For Hegel, this was the *telos* (end goal) of history; for Marx, civil society was merely a stage towards the *telos* of communism.

The contemporary versions of civil society all have normative goals, which can only be fully explained in the context of globalization. The neoliberal version is about the benefits of Western, especially American, society; thus the goal is the spread of this type of society to the rest of the world. Globalization, the spread of global capitalism, is viewed as a positive development, the vehicle, supplemented by global civil society, for achieving global Westernization or 'the end of history'.

The postmodern version has to be related to the break with modernity of which a key component was the nation-state. Even though the postmodernists are anti-teleological, they would see the contestation that is currently taking place on a global scale as a way of breaking with grand narratives, teleological political pro-jects that were associated with states. The rise of the Internet allows for a riot of virtuality and for a denial of the existence of something called the real.

The activist version is about political emancipation. It is about the empowerment of individuals and the extension of democracy. I will argue that war and the threat of war always represented a limitation on democracy. Globalization offers the possibility of overcoming that limitation and, at the same time, the global

extension of democracy has become, as a consequence of globalization, the necessary condition for political emancipation. For
activists, globalization is not an unqualified benefit. It offers possibilities for emancipation on a global scale. But in practice, it
involves growing inequality and insecurity and new forms of violence. Global civil society, for the activists, therefore, is about
'civilizing' or democratizing globalization, about the process
through which groups, movements and individuals can demand
a global rule of law, global justice and global empowerment.
Global civil society does, of course, in my own version, include
those who are opposed to globalization and those who do not see
the need for regulation. Thus my version of global civil society is
based on the belief that a genuinely free conversation, a rational
critical dialogue, will favour the 'civilizing' option.

Organization of the book

These arguments are elaborated in this book. Chapter 2 is about
the civil society literature. I trace the evolution of the concept and
show how the territorially bound concept was limited by war and
by the notion of the non-civilized 'other'. I develop my own
definition of civil society as the medium through which social
contracts or bargains between the individual and the centres of
political and economic power are negotiated, discussed and medi-
ated. I argue that the changing meanings of civil society have to be
understood in terms of the changing character of political authority and the changing content of the contract. In particular, as long
as the contract was negotiated with the territorial state, readiness
to die in war was usually a central obligation exchanged for certain
individual rights.

In chapter 3, I describe the dialogue between the West European peace movement and the East European opposition and
I argue that the concept of global civil society emerged out of
that dialogue. The concept expressed the various global transformations taking place at that time, which eroded the territorial
boundedness of civil society. In particular, I argue that the social
contract associated with the blocs as a form of political authority
was breaking down – a contract that involved huge gains in social
and economic emancipation in exchange for agreeing to the risk
of dying in a nuclear war – and that the difference between

societies based on a form of social contract or political bargain and societies based on coercion was collapsing.

Chapter 4 is about the advent of global politics in the aftermath of the 1989 revolutions. The end of global conflict allows for the domestication of international relations and the participation of citizens, and citizens groups at an international level, along with states and international institutions – for politics, that is to say, social bargaining, instead of diplomacy and war. I describe the various civil society actors engaged in global politics and the various strands of opinion that characterize global politics, reflecting the different contemporary versions of civil society described above. I argue that global civil society in the 1990s was dominated by NGOs, which I describe as 'tamed' social movements and by nationalist and fundamentalist movements, and this gave prominence to neoliberal and postmodern understandings of global civil society. Towards the end of the 1990s, the emergence of the so-called anti-globalization movement has revived the activist content to the term, especially after September 11.

In chapter 5, I argue that global civil society has to be understood in the context of an emerging framework of global governance that includes international organizations as well as states, and in which states are transformed from unilateralist war-making states to multilateralist law-making states. Underpinning any new set of global social contracts is public security – the global extension of domestic security, which necessarily involves the construction of a global rule of law. I describe the new forms of warfare that have emerged in the post-1989 period and how these circumscribe the activities of global civil society in political rather than territorial ways. And I also describe the fundamental changes in the norms concerning human rights and humanitarian intervention as a consequence of pressure from NGOs and social movements as well as the new post-Cold War cooperation. The challenge nowadays is how to control war, and this has to be done through strengthening the framework of international humanitarian law and through reconceptualizing military force as international law enforcement, a sort of international policing, which is more robust than traditional peacekeeping. This is a necessary condition for 'civilizing' globalization. The role of global civil society in a system of global governance is not a substitute for democracy at a national level, but rather should be viewed as a supplement in an era when classical democracy is weakened in the context of globalization.

The final chapter applies these arguments to the post-September 11 conundrum. Does September 11 betoken the end of global civil society – a return to the world of the Great Divide? Or is there, and of course I argue that there is, a crucial role for global civil society in a world where attempts to reimpose the Great Divide can only lead to continuing violence?

One of the main objections to the concept of global civil society is that it represents a new ideology or utopia and that, in particular, it represents a Western liberal-individualist project. Hann and Dunn suggest that the concept is based on a 'fundamental ethnocentricity', which involves an 'impoverished understanding of social relationships'.[15] Brown argues that global civil society is unlikely because in many parts of the world, prosperity and order are valued above freedom.[16]

Two possible answers might be used to counter this objection. One is, unashamedly, that human societies need utopias to avoid the retreat into anomie or even nihilism. In a sense, we could be said to be caught between the barbarism of past utopias (fascism and communism) and the barbarism associated with the absence of utopias – the descent into incivility.

The other related argument draws on some of the elements of the postmodern version, in particular the self-reflexive character of the term global civil society. Civil society is a process, not an end-point. Moreover, it is a contested process. Even in the activist version, it is not a utopian blueprint or model. It is better described as a 'horizon'.[17] It was reinvented, not in the West, but in Eastern Europe and Latin America. And although Western voices are often dominant, the whole idea is one of openness to different perspectives and different modes of emancipation. It is true that many activists are tempted to abandon the concept because of the way it has been co-opted and 'flattened out' by the neoliberals.[18] It is also true that the postmodern version of the concept allows a retreat to communalism, which can often be patriarchal and repressive. But the concept of civil society does start from the assumption that individual freedom is a condition for emancipation both political and economic and, perhaps because of the way the concept has been co-opted, it is a term that offers the possibility of opening up access for the individual to global centres of power. In a sense, the term offers a future direction, which is not dictated.

2
The Discourse of Civil Society

Adam Ferguson, in his *Essay on the History of Civil Society*, published in 1767, uses the term 'conjecture' to describe the way philosophers imagine a state of nature that accords with their own conceptions and preferences. All the early civil society theorists had their own version of the state of nature. For Thomas Hobbes, famously, it was the 'warre, as is of every man, against every man' a condition of 'continual fear, and danger of violent death' in which 'the life of man is solitary, poor, nasty, brutish and short'.[1] For Locke, the state of nature was more prone to war than civil societies, while for Rousseau, the state of nature was a world in which man lived for his sensual pleasures in a state of idleness, guided both by self-preservation and sympathy for others, where he does not fear death because he has no conception of death and where he has no conception of morality but he does no harm. 'The desire of laying the foundation of a favourite system', says Ferguson, 'or a fond expectation, perhaps, that we may be able to penetrate the secrets of nature, to the very source of existence, have, on this subject, led to many fruitless inquiries, and given rise to wild suppositions. Among the various qualities which mankind possesses, we select one or a few particulars on which to establish a theory...'[2]

Something similar could be said about the way in which the contemporary usage of civil society selects concepts which most accord with political or theoretical presuppositions. 'Civil society' has a long conceptual history stretching back to classical antiquity. The meaning of the term and the significance of its use have varied according to historical context and, in particular, the form of political authority. Thus the contemporary theorist has an array of concepts from which to derive her or his own version. 'Remembering the dead', as John Keane puts it,[3] is always selective; it necessarily involves forgetting as well.

Although the concept of civil society was based on universalistic ideas, that is to say on notions of human equality, it was historically caught up with a territorially bound form of political authority. One of my concerns in this chapter is to investigate the implications of this territorial boundedness. If we are to find ways in which the term can be reconceptualized so as to be applicable in a more globalized context, we need to think about how civil society concepts relate to the world beyond the territory of the state.

In what follows, I shall start with a thumbnail sketch of the changing meanings of civil society concepts over time and how they relate to the evolution of forms of political authority and, in particular, to state formation. I then consider two aspects of the territorially bounded nature of the concept: the relation to war and the relation to 'non civil' societies. In the final section, I will develop my own definition of civil society, drawing (necessarily selectively) on those elements of classical concepts (using the term 'classical' to refer to great thinkers and not to antiquity) that seem most relevant to a usage of civil society that can be applied both in relation to the territorial state and to deterritorialized forms of political authority.

Meanings of civil society

The term 'civil society' has always been associated with the formation of a particular type of political authority. But the ambiguity of the concept arises from its changing meaning over time. This changing meaning arises from several factors: the changing content or coverage of the term – what it was not; the tension between normative and descriptive, idealistic and empiricist, subjective and objective implications of the concept; and the relative emphasis on the private and the public or the individual and the social.

Content or coverage

For seventeenth- and eighteenth-century thinkers, civil society was defined in contrast to the state of nature. Civil society was a society characterized by the rule of law, based on certain fundamental individual rights, which was enforced by a political authority also subject to the rule of law. Indeed there was no clear distinction at that time between civil society and the state. Rather civil society was a generic term for a secular constitutional order.[4]

The term came to prominence during the transition from absolutist monarchies to the modern state, although it had a prehistory in ancient and medieval times. This was a period when earlier ties of blood, kinship and religion were breaking down. With the development of what Giddens calls time–space distanciation[5] new more abstract forms of social interaction supplanted the personal face-to-face relations that characterized local communities. The growth of states and the establishment of a rule of law gradually eliminated private and often violent methods of settling disputes and created the conditions for these new forms of social interaction based on commonly accepted but impersonal means of communication, e.g. exchanges of money, newspapers, mail etc.

The term was linked to the concept of 'civility'.[6] It meant respect for individual autonomy, based on security and trust among people who had perhaps never met. It required regularity of behaviour, rules of conduct, respect for law, and control of violence. Hence, a civil society was synonymous with polite society, a society in which strangers act in a civilized way towards each other, treating each other with mutual respect, tolerance and confidence, a society in which rational debate and discussion becomes possible. Norbert Elias referred to the 'civilising process' to describe the historical process whereby violence was removed from everyday life.[7] Emma Rothschild talks about the 'unfrightened mind' – the removal of fear, which provides the source of superstition.[8]

By and large, civil societies were associated with those forms of political authority that were beginning to displace the absolutist monarchies in Europe. They were societies characterized by what were then described as republican constitutions, in which monarchs or rulers were accountable to some form of legislature. Although the term civil society was not distinguished from the state, the importance of checking state power as a condition for civil society was given emphasis from the seventeenth century onwards. Unlike Hobbes, who saw security or internal pacification as the fundamental characteristic of civil society, something which was compatible with a powerful state (a Leviathan), Locke insisted that absolute monarchy could not be equated with civil government. For him, supreme power was based on the legislature; the separation of the legislature from the executive, as well as the right of free public expression were conditions for civil society. Juridical equality applied both to rulers and the ruled. 'When a King has dethroned himself and put himself in a state of war with his people, what shall hinder them from prosecuting him who is King, as they would any other man, who has put himself in a state of war with them?'[9]

It was also Locke who was the first to introduce the notion of private property as a condition for civil society. Locke developed an argument about private property as a fundamental right based on the idea that a man possesses his own labour and if he adds his labour to the products of nature, he takes possession of those products. This notion was later to be elaborated by the Scottish enlightenment thinkers, particularly Adam Smith, who stressed the development of a market economy as the basis for civil or civilized society.

The distinction between civil society and the state, that is to say the shift from civil society defined in contrast to the state of nature to civil society defined in contrast to the state, is associated with the rise of what Tilly calls the national state[10] in the late eighteenth and nineteenth centuries. This involved a growth in the functions, extensiveness and centralization of state power, a shift in the status of individuals from subjects to citizens, and an increase in the extent of democratic control, at least on paper, over states. This was the period when state bureaucracy was developed and when various public institutions were established – central banks, professional armies, the education system – clearly separated from the private interests of rulers. It was Hegel who, strongly influenced by the Scottish political economists, defined civil society as 'the realm of difference, intermediate between the family and the state'.[11] In other words, civil society was equated with bourgeois society (*Bürgerliche Gesellschaft*) and included the market; this was the definition to be taken up by Marx and later nineteenth-century thinkers. For Hegel, famously, civil society was 'the achievement of the modern world . . . the territory of mediation where there is free play for every idiosyncrasy, every talent, every accident of birth and fortune, and where waves of passion gush forth, regulated only by reason, glinting through them'.[12]

Thus civil society was the realm of contradiction and the modern state was conceived by Hegel as a mediator, as an expression of the reconciliation of the tensions in civil society. The employees of the state, the civil servants and the professional military, were defined as a universal class, who act on behalf of the public good. For this reason, many later scholars have considered that the Hegelian concept overemphasizes the role of the state as the guarantor of civil society. Cohen and Arato, in their monumental work on civil society and political theory, rehabilitate the Hegelian concept. They point out that the authority of local communities and of what were called corporations (guilds or associations) in civil society are considered to be the 'barrier against the intrusion of subjective caprice into the power entrusted to the civil servant'.[13] Civil society was the arena through which the individual was socialized; through working with others within the institutions of civil society, the individual became conscious of 'universal ends'. According to Cohen and Arato: 'Like Montesquieu before him and Tocqueville after him, he sought an intermediate level of power between individual and the state; he feared the powerlessness of atomised subjects and sought to control the potential arbitrariness of the state bureaucracy.'[14]

Although de Tocqueville did not use the term civil society, his contribution needs to be mentioned because of the importance he attributed to associationalism and self-organization, which was to inform so much of contemporary thinking. In his study of democracy as practised in America, de Tocqueville argued that the guarantee of individual liberties was to be found in what he called 'democratic expedients'; these included local self-government, the separation of Church and State, a free press, indirect elections, an independent judiciary and, above all, 'associational life'.[15] In America, he was greatly impressed by the extent of associations in civil life and put forward the argument that those active associations were a condition for freedom and equality. As the state takes over more and more functions of daily life, as the division of labour becomes more complex and as demands for the redistribution of wealth increase, an active voluntary sector is necessary to provide a check on state power.

> As soon as several inhabitants of the United States have taken up an opinion or a feeling they wish to promote in the world, they look for mutual assistance; and as soon as they have found one another out, they combine. From that moment they are no longer isolated men, but a power seen from afar, whose actions serve for example and whose language is listened to ... Among the laws that rule human societies, there is one which seems to be more precise and clear than all the others. If men are to remain civilised or to become so, the art of associating together must grow and improve in the same ratio as the equality of conditions is increased.[16]

For Marx and Engels, political associations were a reflection of material conditions. They were to take up the Hegelian concept of *Bürgerliche Gesellschaft* and to emphasize the role of the econ-omy. According to Marx, the 'material conditions of life are summed up by Hegel after the fashion of the English and the French of the eighteenth century under the name "civil society"; the anatomy of civil society is to be sought in political economy'.[17] Unlike Hegel, however, Marx and Engels argued that the state was subordinate to civil society; they saw the state as an instrument or apparatus in the hands of the dominant classes. Civil society was the 'theatre of history... Civil Society embraces all the material relations of individuals within a definite stage of the development of productive forces. It embraces the whole commercial and industrial life of a given stage and, hence, transcends the State and the nation, though, on the other hand again, it must assert itself in its foreign relations as nationality and inwardly must organise itself as state.'[18]

In the twentieth century, the content of the concept has been further narrowed to forms of social interaction that are distinct from both the state and the market. Writing in prison, the Italian Marxist Gramsci called into question the economism of the Marx-ist definition of civil society. According to Gramsci, it is not 'economic structure' as such that governs political action but the 'interpretation of it'. Thus the 'theatre of history' is not the story of economic development but of ideological and cultural strug-gles. Gramsci drew an important distinction between coercion and consent, domination and hegemony. Bourgeois society had established a powerful set of norms and institutions to sustain the hegemony of bourgeois rule based on the consent of the working classes. Whereas capitalism was overthrown in Russia through the capture of the state, this was not possible in the West where 'there was a proper relation between state and civil society, and when the state trembled, a sturdy structure of civil society was at once revealed'.[19] Hence, he was to emphasize the need for political activism in the realms of education, media and other institutions of civil society.

In contemporary usage, the term tends to refer to social movements, associations, NGOs or the non-profit sector. As the term emerged in Eastern Europe and Latin America, the emphasis was on self-organization and civic autonomy in reaction to the vast increase in the reach of the modern state, and on the creation of independent spaces, in which individuals can act according to their consciences in the face of powerful influences from the state on culture and ideology. This concept was taken up by Western radicals who saw civil society as a check both on the power and arbitrariness of the contemporary state and on the power of unbridled capitalism. Those who had favoured stronger states to resolve the contradictions generated by capitalism had failed to anticipate the dangers of an overbearing state. According to Habermas:

> The expression 'civil society' has in the meantime taken on a meaning different from that of the 'bourgeois society' of the liberal tradition, which Hegel conceptualised as the 'system of needs', that is, as a market system involving social labour and commodity exchange. What is meant by 'civil society' today, in contrast to its usage in the Marxist tradition, no longer includes the economy as constituted by private law and steered through markets in labour, capital and commodities. Rather, its institutional core comprises those non-governmental and non-economic connections and voluntary associations that anchor the communication structures of the public sphere in the society component of the life-world. Civil society is composed of those more or less spontaneously emergent associations, organisations, and movements that, attuned to how societal problems resonate in private life spheres, distil and transmit such reactions to the public sphere. The core of civil society comprises a network of associations that institutionalises problem-solving discourses of general interest inside the framework of organised public spheres. These 'discursive designs' have an

egalitarian, open form of organisation that mirrors essential features of the kind of communication around which they crystallise and to which they lend continuity and permanence.[20]

For many radicals who share this Habermasian understanding of civil society, the term no longer excludes the family. Historically, the exclusion of the family reflected the male nature of citizenship. The women's movement of the 1970s and 1980s typified the new form of organization described by Habermas and the re-invented civil society seemed to be a sphere of politics particularly suited to women's engagement. The extension of rights to cover issues like domestic violence or the repression of homosexuality has been an important dimension of the contemporary version of civil society.[21]

There is also, of course, a more establishment view in which civil society is considered more passively, less as a check on the state and on capitalism and more as a complement to or even substitute for the state and the market, a way of smoothing the path of market reform and implementing state programmes, what I have described as the neoliberal version. Civil society, according to this line of thought, is the realm between the state, the market and the family, but it is a realm of stability rather than struggle, of service provision rather than advocacy, of trust and responsibility rather than emancipation.[22] Terms like not-for-profit or non-governmental organizations describe the actors of civil society rather than the social movements or protest groups that inhabit the more activist version of civil society. Fukuyama's writings on trust or Robert Putnam's ideas about social capital have contributed to this conception of civil society.[23]

Normative versus descriptive approaches

The second factor has to do with the tension between the normative and descriptive signification of the concept, something that has swung back and forth over time, and remains a subject of contention. Is civil society the *telos* (end goal) of the social organization of human beings (Aristotle), an aspiration for politically minded individuals? Or is civil society merely a description of what exists, with good or bad features depending on one's perspective? And, further, is the evolution of civil society determined – is it the result of the natural working out of history? Or does it depend on the will of human beings and is it, therefore, reversible?

The early modern theorists (seventeenth- and eighteenth-century) drew the concept of civil society from their readings of the Greek philosophers, who used the term *politike koinona* (political society/community) which was translated into Latin as *societas civilis*. For the ancients, the concept had a strong moral content. It was a law-governed society in which the law was seen as the expression of public virtue, the Aristotelian 'good life'. Civilization was thus linked to a particular form of political power, in which rulers put the public good before private interest. Indeed Plato in *The Republic* envisages a state which brings private passions and interests under control.[24] For Aristotle, the *polis*, which was more or less synonymous with civil society, was the *telos* of man as a political animal. It was through political action and public deliberation, through the public use of reason, that ethical life was realized.

What distinguished the early modern thinkers from their predecessors was their emphasis on human equality. Men were seen as autonomous individuals, who possessed fundamental rights by virtue of being human. They imagined a state of nature, that is to say, a situation characterized by the absence of political authority or law, in which individuals were free to pursue their private interests. The different Fergusonian 'conjectures' about the state of nature depended on assumptions about the fundamental character of human beings, whether individuals are naturally guided by self-preservation (Hobbes) or whether they are also motivated by 'moral sentiments and natural affections' (Locke).[25] Central to the early modern theorists was the notion of a social contract, a hypothetical device, which expressed an underlying reality, used to explain the constitution of civil society. Through the social contract, men (and for the early modern thinkers it was men and not women) exchanged their freedom for rights guaranteed under a civil law.[26] For Hobbes, the fundamental right was security. For Locke, it was also liberty and, above all, property that were guaranteed by law.

For seventeenth-century thinkers, law-governed political authority, as it was for the ancients, was an expression of public morality. Civil law had a moral basis in the law of nature, which men, through the use of reason, were beginning to discover. Civil society was an ethical arena, a realm of public morality, based on individual conscience. The early thinkers, strongly influenced by Calvinism, believed that this ethical arena was based on a divine underpinning, that knowledge of what was right and wrong was imprinted by God in individual consciousness. It was immanent in nature, whose author was God.[27] Later, as secular morality came to supplant religious injunction, this public realm was understood to be held together by nature, the notion that natural behaviour is learned, and that through experience men come to understand that altruistic behaviour sustains the public realm which is required for individual autonomy.

The Scottish enlightenment thinkers were the first to talk about civil society not as an ideal but a living reality and, in so doing, they broke the link between nature and public morality. The Scottish enlightenment thinkers were the first to apply the methods of natural science to the study of society and to argue that our knowledge depends not on subjective theorizing but on facts, especially history and economy. They developed a stadial theory of history, which was to be taken up by Hegel and Marx, whereby society developed through different stages defined in terms of 'modes of subsistence', methods of producing basic needs.[28] Civil society was still defined as a society characterized by the rule of the law and restrictions on the use of violence in social relations. But it was no longer contrasted with the state of nature. Rather civil society is what exists; it is viewed as a consequence of the evolution of society which could be understood not through 'conjecture' but rather through an empirical study of the actual history of mankind and through the observation of 'rude' nations. 'We speak of art as distinguished from nature' says Ferguson 'but art itself is natural to man. He is in some measure the artifice of his own frame, as well as his fortune, and is destined from the first age of his being to invent and contrive . . . . If we are asked therefore, Where is the state of nature to be found? We may answer, It is here: and it matters not whether we are understood to speak in the island of Great Britain, at the Cape of Good Hope, or the Straits of Magellan. . . . What the savage projects or observes, in the forest, are the steps which led nations, more advanced, from the architecture of the cottage to that of the palace, and conducted the human mind from the perceptions of sense, to the general conclusions of science.'[29]

Ferguson's essay was entitled a 'history of civil society'. His study of what he called the 'rude' nations was based on his own travels, especially to North America. History, in his view, did lead to civilization partly because of the advance of technology and increased wealth and partly because of man's natural tendencies for affection towards his fellow human beings, which he observed among the 'rude' nations. For him individualism was a modern condition – a consequence of commercial society. Man had always lived in groups and Ferguson's study of history and other societies seems to indicate that human beings are motivated not only by self-preservation but also by love, courage, generosity and honour. It is only in commercial society 'if ever, that man is sometimes found a detached and solitary being; he has found an object which sets him in competition with his fellow-creatures, and he deals with them as he does with his cattle and his soil, for the sake of the profits they bring'.[30] Moreover, among the 'rude' nations, according to Ferguson, are to be found many qualities that are lacking in civil society.[31]

The implication of this way of reasoning is that civil society is not necessarily superior in moral terms to the 'rude' nations. There is no natural tendency towards progress although progress does take place as a result of conscious moral efforts. The constitution of civil society cannot be derived from a formal blueprint. It is the outcome of a process rather than a contract – a process that is, at least in part, the consequence of public pressures. It is the unanticipated consequence of a medley of human developments in which innate moral sentiments for social action play a critical part, the end result of various social currents, a compromise between contending parties. The 'influence of laws, where they have any real effect in the preservation of liberties, is not in any magic power descended from shelves that are loaded with books but is, in reality, the influence of men resolved to be free; of men, who having adjusted in writing the terms on which they live with the state, and with their fellow-subjects, are determined, by their vigilance and spirit, to make these terms be observed'.[32]

The normative content of the concept of civil society was to be reconstructed by Kant in the late eighteenth century, at least in part in response to the thinking of the Scottish enlightenment. For Kant, morality could be derived from reason in a way that was independent of actual experience and it was this moral autonomy that provided the basis for freedom, and which offered the possibility to overcome concrete historical conditions. Through enlightenment, man emerges from 'self-incurred immaturity' where immaturity is understood as the 'inability to use one's own understanding without the guidance of another'.[33] Kant's categorical imperative to act in a way that could be applied as a universal law provided a basis for fundamental human rights. The term 'community of ends' referred to the idea that the individual human being is an end in her or himself, and that this provides the organizing principle of civil society. As was the case for earlier theorists, public debate and public expression were of great importance in developing a rational basis for law and for political authority. Public enlightenment, that is to say, the 'freedom to make *public use* of one's reason in all matters',[34] is the condition for the realization of a 'community of ends'.

Universal civil society is indeed the *telos* of human development but it is attained not through some prearranged rational plan nor through instinct but rather an antagonistic process of learning through experience, through the conflict between man as a private being guided by selfish interests and man as a rational moral being, which is expressed in public discord. Kant uses the term *'asocial sociability* of man' to describe the 'tendency to come together in society, coupled however with a continual resistance which constantly threatens to break society up ... Man has an inclination to *live in society*, since he feels in this state more like a man, that is, he feels able to develop his natural capacities. But he also has a great tendency to *live as an individual*, to isolate himself, since he also encounters in himself the unsocial characteristic of wanting to direct everything in accordance with his own ideas.'[35] It is this tension between man as a moral being and his asocial qualities that transforms 'the primitive natural capacity for moral discrimination into definite practical principles; and thus a *pathologically* enforced social union is transformed into a *moral* whole'.[36]

It was Hegel who effected a synthesis between the more formalistic morality of Kant and the empirical tradition of the Scottish enlightenment, developing a purposive theory of history based on the workings out of the contradictions between subjective and objective, reason and passion, the particular and the general. As was the case with the ancient Greeks, the state became the expression of the public good, although modern society is distinguished from ancient society in the notion of subjective freedom. Hegel criticized the Kantian notion that reason could be expressed *a priori*; rather reason is the consequence of actual practice. *Sittlichkeit* (ethical life) is the 'institutionalisation or actualisation of freedom'.[37] Civil society as the 'achievement of the modern world' is the unintended and unanticipated outcome of a historical process, in which a developed market economy enables the reconciliation of private wants, and public freedom allows the realization of morality.

Marx and Engels were to build on Hegel's dialectical approach. But for them, civil society was not the *telos* of history but a stage towards the *telos* of communism in which the distinction between state and civil society would wither away. Political freedom was bourgeois freedom. Without economic emancipation, it was, at best, a stage in the development of mankind, and, at worst, a smokescreen, or as Gellner puts it, a 'fraud and an illusion'.[38] This is an argument that continues to be put forward by left critics of the concept of civil society.[39]

The tension between the normative and the descriptive continues to pervade contemporary usage. For Western establishment thinkers, civil society remains the *telos* of human development but this *telos* already exists now in the West – this is Fukuyama's 'End of History' thesis. For more radical thinkers, civil society is what exists today in the realm between the state and the economy – a terrain of contestation and conflict, characterized by inequality, fundamentalism and reaction, as well as progressive social movements. For Arato and Cohen, who have theorized the notion of civil society as a contemporary emancipatory project, the term combines the normative and the descriptive. They see civil society as a form of Habermasian communicative action – an actual process of deliberation through which individuals can establish the validity of moral claims. Thus Kantian formalism is supplanted by a deliberative procedure which is realized through the reality of public discord and debate that is experienced in civil society. Civil society is a way of countering what Habermas calls the 'colonisation' of the 'life-world' both by capitalism and by communism. In a parallel fashion, the East Europeans envisaged civil society as a form of enlightenment, in which individuals can 'live in truth' (Havel) or, in other words, act according to reasoned morality and not the dictates of the totalitarian state.

Public versus private

A third factor that contributes to the ambiguity of the concept of civil society is the differing relative emphasis on the public versus private realms, the individual versus the community. All modern theories of civil society derive from a notion of individual autonomy and human equality that emerged in the transition to modernity as ascribed social rankings were swept away. The theories of civil society developed by the philosophers of antiquity placed the emphasis on public virtue and lacked the notion of private or subjective freedom. For contemporary liberals, it is the achievement of private freedom or negative liberty that was the 'miracle of civil society'.[40] Gellner applauds the fact that civil society allows the individual the freedom to be disengaged; he or she is not forced to have an opinion or to participate in public life. He argues that Marxism failed, above all, because it lacked a concept of the profane; there was no private space in which to be ordinary. 'The splendid thing about Civil Society is that even the absent-minded, or those preoccupied with their private concerns or for any other reason ill-suited to the exercise of eternal and intimidating vigilance, can look forward to enjoying their liberty . . . Civil Society is an order in which liberty . . . is available to the timorous, non-vigilant and absent-minded.'[41]

For others, however, there was always the danger that the retreat to private concerns would lead to authoritarianism. Private freedom could be guaranteed only if it were combined with public virtue or positive liberty. The early modern theorists resolved this tension through the device of the social contract, which presupposed that moral autonomy did not only mean possessive individualism. But for those who rejected the formalism of the contractual approach or of the Kantian resolution, public virtue was by no means assured. Thus, Ferguson's essay, for example, could be read as a warning about the dangers contained in civil society. Since Ferguson rejects the contractual approach of Hobbes and Locke, and since man's natural sociability, which he observes among the 'rude' nations, is transformed in civil society into legalistic duties, his theory of civil society contains no automatic formula for social cohesion. He fears, above all, a retreat to privatism, apathy and passivity – he is concerned about the risks of corruption and about the danger of a new tyranny or despotism based on the satisfaction of private needs. He also fears that the division of labour when applied to politics will lead to a separate military class, that the individual citizen will lose his commitment to public virtue if he is not required to defend his country, and that the military could usurp their position. Thus like many other thinkers of the period, he appeals to a classical idea of civic virtue, using the model of Sparta to offset the private concerns that are characteristic of commercial society. 'Men are qualified to receive this blessing [liberty], only in proportion as they are made to apprehend their own rights; and are made to respect the just pretensions of mankind; in proportion as they are willing to sustain, in their own persons, the burden of government and of national defence; and are willing to prefer the engagements of a liberal mind, to the enjoyments of sloth, or the delusive hope of a safety purchased by submission and fear.'[42]

Similar concerns are expressed by de Tocqueville. For de Tocqueville, the moving principle of democracy is equality. He fears that equality could lead to tyranny as well as to democracy. He chose to study democracy in America because this was the society nearest to the 'actualisation of equality' not only in equal opportunities and the assurance of political rights but also 'in a general levelling of wealth'. The problem is that equality can also mean atomism. The classes of the old regime have been destroyed; how to create artificial ties that can replace the traditional bonds of the middle ages?

> Around the issue of individualism will be seen to cluster certain propensities, which together give rise to what we may call the problem of democracy. These are the passion for well being and material comforts, a concern for one's private welfare to the exclusion of all consideration of public affairs, and an inevitable drift towards mediocrity. They make democratic man all too prone to accept or drift into a despotism securing him these pursuits and preferences. A resolution of the problem of democracy entails finding a place for liberty, for human excellence, for the re-emergence of public virtue, and for the possibility of greatness.[43]

Like Ferguson, de Tocqueville is also concerned about the risks of military intervention in politics, once the military become a separate class.

This fear of the destructive consequences of individualism was not universally shared. Others argued that the dissolution of the old order allowed for a higher form of association in which men and women could come together through 'natural sympathy' instead of the exclusive, non-voluntary ties that characterized traditional society, thereby generating a new set of public *mœurs*.[44] In the new commercial society, the 'indifferent stranger' replaced suspicious outsider. Emma Rothschild points out that thinkers like Adam Smith and David Hume, or Condorcet in France, were more confident about the capacity of individuals to understand each other through civilized political conversation. Their world, like today's world, was a world of uncertainty and the 'virtue which contributes to legal and constitutional security is, for Smith and Hume, a very modest condition. Like the domestic virtues, or the conversations about gratitude and remorse, which constitute the system of moral sentiments, it is an unheroic sort of heroism.'[45] What is required, according to this line of thought, is not 'vigilance' or 'greatness', rather it is public discourse. 'The discursive political society, or the philosophical politics of good-tempered discussion, requires a society of good-tempered, prudent, moral sentiments; this is the condition for civilised conflict.'[46] These thinkers had 'faith, of a sort, in the ordinary virtues of conversation, and in the ordinary exchanges of political discussion. They believed... that individuals in commercial societies longed for individual independence, and not, like de Tocqueville, that they were frozen in individual isolation.'[47]

To some extent, the concept of civil society developed by Habermas and by Arato and Cohen reflects this idea of civilized political conversation. 'In short, rights do not only secure negative liberty, the autonomy of private, disconnected individuals,' say Arato and Cohen. 'They also secure the autonomous (freed from state control) communicative interaction of individuals with one another in the public and private spheres of civil society, as well as a new relation of individuals to the public, and the political spheres of society and the state.'[48] At the same time, however, they echo the more muscular concern about the need to overcome the tendencies for civil 'privatism' or egoism, which have followed the collapse of socialist ideologies in the West as well as the East and they see the revival of 'civil society' as a 'political project' and 'action-orienting norm', although not as a new utopia.[49]

Ferguson's understanding of civil society is a male-dominated, patriarchal version of the concept. The divide between active and passive citizenship, or between positive and negative freedom, parallels another interpretation of the public/private divide, that between civil society and the family. Feminists reject the public/private divide since the family can be an oppressive, violent sphere. The politicization of domestic issues through civil society opens up much greater possibilities for the emancipation of women. And the understanding of civil society as one, which overcomes the public/private divide through reason and interaction, offers greater possibility for 'civilizing' public affairs.

Civil society and war

Despite the differences I have described, all modern concepts of civil society share the presupposition that the basis for civil society is the rule of law, which applies both to rulers and the ruled and which is underpinned by a set of shared public norms, individual rights and free public expression. Up to now, however, civil society has always been a territorially bounded concept contiguous with the territorial sway of the state, although this boundedness was less evident in the earlier period. As I have described, the emergence of the concept was linked to the formation of states and the centralization of political power in a given territory. This centralization of power was, at the same time, concomitant with the fragmentation of power in the international arena. The Treaty of Westphalia of 1648 marked not only the mutual recognition of the sovereignty and autonomy of secular rulers; it also marked the breakdown of the universal authority of the Church in Europe.[50] Thus the international arena was said to be characterized by the state of nature or anarchy since there was no international rule of law and no overarching political authority.

A recurrent theme in both civil society and international relations thinking has been the importance of war as a condition for civil society. Ian Clark talks about the Great Divide to describe the way this dichotomy between war and civil society or anarchy versus rule-based systems has dominated the main theoretical approaches of international relations.[51] Thus Martin Wight pointed to the contrast between the 'good life' within the national state and the struggle for survival without. Rob Walker argues that 'inside the particular state, concepts of obligation, freedom, and justice could be articulated within the context of universalist accounts ... Yet these claims to universal values and processes presumed ... a boundary beyond which such universals could not be guaranteed.'[52]

There are various versions of this argument about the Great Divide. The first has to do with the necessity to concentrate the means of violence in the hands of the state in order to remove violence from domestic relations. What Norbert Elias called the 'civilising process' – the removal of violence from everyday life within the boundaries of the state – was based on the establishment of monopolies of violence and taxation. 'The society of what we call the modern age is characterised, above all in the West, by a certain level of monopolisation. Free use of weapons is denied the individual and reserved to a central authority of whatever kind, and likewise, the taxation of property or income of individuals is concentrated in the hands of a central social authority. The financial means thus flowing into this central authority maintain its monopoly of force, while this, in turn, maintains the monopoly of taxation. Neither has in any sense precedence over the other; they are two sides of the same monopoly.'[53]

A crucial point about this monopoly process was the balance between the interests of the ruler (private) and the interests of the members of what Elias called 'state-regulated society' (public). The shift from a private to a public monopoly, from absolutism to the nation-state or national state, was part of the process of state-building and of concentrating the means of violence and of taxation; for it required a complex and specialized administrative apparatus and social interdependence, which in turn restricted the power of the ruler.

The construction of these monopolies was, as Tilly has shown, intimately bound up with war against other states.[54] On the one hand, the establishment of central authority was built up through eliminating domestic military competition, as a consequence of civil war and the experience of civil war. On the other hand, interstate war became the only legitimate form of organized violence and, moreover, was sharply distinguished from peace. In place of more or less continuous warfare, war became a discrete episode that was reserved for use against other states and was excluded from internal relations. Domestic pacification (the elimination of private armies, the reduction of corruption, violent crime, piracy and brigandage), the growth of taxation and public borrowing, the regularization of armed forces and police forces, the development of nationalist sentiment, were all mutually reinforcing in wartime. At the same time, the expanded capacity for warfare greatly increased the potential for destruction. Elias, writing on the eve of the Second World War, was fearful of the barbarity that could be unleashed by so-called civilized nations.

Although war was important for all states, Tilly distinguishes between coercion-intensive and capital-intensive modes of development. Cities were associated with capital and coercion was concentrated in states. 'Where capital defines a realm of exploitation, coercion defines a realm of domination.'[55] Where cities were strong, states sought funding for their coercive apparatus through a process of negotiation with capitalists – the most extreme case being the Dutch Republic composed of a federation of largely autonomous city states. Where cities were weak, as in the Eastern empires, military structures were constructed through domestic coercion. According to this line of thought, it was the bargaining process linked to war-making in capital-intensive societies that allowed for the construction of a domestic civil society. Tilly describes the evolution of the bargaining process as it changed over time starting with the 'suppression of popular insurrections against taxation or conscription' and later taking

> more acceptable forms: pleading with parliaments, buying off city officials with tax exemptions, confirming guild privileges in return for loans and fees, regularising the assessment and collection of taxes against the guarantee of their more willing payment and so on. All this bargaining created or confirmed individual and collective claims on the state, individual and collective rights vis-à-vis the state, and obligations of the state to its citizens. It also created rights – recognised enforceable claims – of states with respect to their citizens. The core of what we call 'citizenship', indeed, consists of multiple bargains hammered out by rulers and the ruled in the course of their struggles over the means of state action, especially the making of war.[56]

A second argument about the Great Divide relates to the importance of instilling a sense of patriotism and civic duty as a way of sustaining social solidarity in an individualistic society. This was a significant strand in the thinking of Adam Ferguson. Associated with the monopolization of violence was a change in the nature of war. Wars became less frequent, and, up to the twentieth century, it was argued often that wars were fought more humanely. The so-called Western Way of War was characterized by set-piece battles and by decisive encounters in the name of state interest.[57] Adam Ferguson echoed the thinking of many of his contemporaries in arguing that civil societies were more

concerned with the pursuit of wealth than making war, in contrast
to monarchies, although their capacity to make and win wars was
greatly enhanced:

> Glory is more successfully obtained by saving and protecting, than
> by destroying the vanquished, and the most amiable of all objects is,
> in appearance, attained; the employing of force only for the
> obtaining of justice, and for the preservation of natural rights.
>
> This is perhaps the principal characteristic, on which, among
> modern nations, we bestow the epithets of *civilised* or of
> polished.[58]

Nevertheless, Ferguson feared the loss of national spirit
that resulted from the division of labour in civil societies and
the creation of a separate military class. And at the same time,
he also feared the scale of war and devastation that might
result from failure to control the military and from excessive
national sentiment.[59] Hence his proposal for citizen-soldiers
along the lines of the Greek city states. A corollary to this
argument was the contrast between civil and martial law. In
wartime, the citizen must be prepared to give up his personal
freedom and to give unquestioning obedience to the military
leadership – for Ferguson, this is 'the most important lesson
of civil society'.[60] Hence the individual character of civil society
was the other side of the coin of the collectivism of civil society as
a whole.

Interestingly, de Tocqueville, despite his emphasis on civic
activism, develops a similar argument. De Tocqueville drew attention to the dangers to democracy of standing armies, who favour
war because it is the best route to military advancement and who
are liable to intervene in domestic affairs. He also considered that
protracted war endangers democracy by increasing the powers of
government and the degree of centralization. Yet at the same time
'war almost always enlarges the mind of a people and raises their
character. In some cases it is the only check to the excessive
growth of certain propensities that naturally spring out of the
equality of conditions, and it must be considered a necessary
corrective to certain inveterate diseases to which democratic communities are liable.'[61] De Tocqueville's solution was not citizen-
soldiers but rather the necessity to infuse the democratic spirit
into military life.

A third and much stronger version of the argument about the link between war and civil society is the proposition of Hegel, later taken up by Marx, that war has a historic mission in the development of the state. For Marx, war was the 'midwife' of a new society. For Hegel, external sovereignty creates the basis of internal authority. Hegel argues that the state is established through crisis and war and that it is only through self-sacrifice that the citizen understands the primacy of the state. Indeed, it is in war rather than the social contract, when the state acts as an individual in relation to other states, that individual freedom and social solidarity are reconciled. For Hegel, this notion of the state as an individual is the basis of his critique of the perpetual peace theories of Rousseau and Kant. War, says Hegel, is necessary to preserve the 'ethical health of peoples . . . Just as the movement of the ocean prevents the corruption which would be the result of perpetual calm, so by war people escape the corruption which would be occasioned by a continuous or eternal peace.'[62] Hegel argues that 'sacrifice for the sake of the individuality of the state is the substantive relation of all the citizens, and is, thus, a universal duty'. Moreover, he claims that 'bravery of civilised peoples' is in fact an expression of freedom:

> The content of bravery as a sentiment is found in the true absolute and final end, the sovereignty of the state. Bravery realises this end, and in so doing gives up personal reality. Hence, in this feeling are found the most rigorous and direct antagonisms. There is present in it a self-sacrifice, which is yet the existence of freedom. In it is found the highest self-control or independence, which yet in its existence submits to the mechanism of an external order and a life of service. An utter obedience or complete abnegation of one's own opinion and reasonings, even an absence of one's own spirit, is coupled with the most intense and comprehensive direct presence of the spirit and of resolution. The most hostile and hence most personal attitude towards individuals is allied with perfect indifference, or even, it may be, a kindly feeling towards them as individuals.[63]

Pierre Hassner, in his seminal essay on Hegel's thought, asks whether there is not a tension between Hegel's insistence on the necessity of war and his notion of the 'end of history'? 'If the sense of war is to be found primarily in the development and diffusion of civilisation, what happens once this development and diffusion have been definitively realised?'[64] Since war waged by civilized nations must be justified in terms of the defence of civilization if it is to have the political and moral educative functions ascribed by Hegel, can there be any justification for war once all nations have reached a similar stage of civilization? But if the 'end of history' means the 'withering away of war' would not that 'decadence, that *Versumpfen der Menschen* which Hegel attributes to pacific civil society continue and reach its end'?[65]

This Hegelian argument was to recur both in populist ideas of nationalism as well as among those who were to provide a legitimating narrative for twentieth-century forms of authoritarianism. For Carl Schmitt, writing in the inter-war period, the notion of the 'political' is essentially related to 'the real physical possibility of killing'. 'According to this theory,' Habermas explains, 'a legally pacified domestic policy must be supplemented by a belligerent foreign policy licensed by international law because the state, which enjoys a monopoly over the means of violence, can only uphold law and order in the face of the virulent force of subversive domestic enemies so long as it preserves and regenerates its political substance in the struggle against external enemies.'[66]

Not all the theorists of civil society took this view. Most liberal political theorists of the eighteenth and nineteenth centuries envisaged the construction of a liberal international order linked to the rise of domestic civil society, in which force was increasingly limited to policing actions, the enforcement of justice, and many developed their own perpetual peace schemes.[67] The best known is Kant's proposal, although he drew on Rousseau's description of the Abbé Saint Pierre's scheme for perpetual peace. Kant took the view that the construction of civil society would necessarily be universalized. Indeed, while he argued that a republican constitution was a condition for perpetual peace, he also thought that a fully functioning civil society was not possible except in the framework of what we would now call a global civil society. According to Kant: 'The problem of establishing a perfect civil society is subordinate to the problem of a law-governed external relationship with other states, and cannot be solved unless the latter is also solved.'[68] War necessarily represented an infringement of civil freedom; it was expensive, destructive and uncertain. Indeed, Rousseau had suggested in his description of the Abbé Saint-Pierre's peace scheme that war was the device through which rulers sustained their power, providing a 'pretext' for taxation and for obedience.[69] The same point had been made by earlier thinkers on war and peace, especially Erasmus.[70]

Kant envisaged three possibilities. One was that, through chance, men would arrive at a form of international arrangement capable of surviving. The second possibility was that nature would lead men in an orderly way to develop a scheme that could govern the peaceful relations between nations. And the third was that 'nothing rational will anywhere emerge from all these actions and counter-actions among men' and that the 'discord which is so natural to our species' may be 'preparing the way for a hell of evils to overtake us' for 'barbaric devastation' which 'might perhaps again destroy this civilised state and all the cultural progress hitherto achieved'.[71]

The experience of the twentieth century seems to suggest that the third possibility was the most realistic and the experience of war and totalitarianism has underlined our scepticism about a teleological view of history and a determined progress towards civil society. As Habermas has pointed out, Kant failed to foresee the rise of nationalism and the way it swamped republican constitutions. He failed to anticipate the contradictions and antagonism that would arise as a consequence of the growth of trade, which Kant argued was a factor contributing to perpetual peace. And he could not possibly have envisaged the twentieth-century 'betrayal of intellectuals' and the way in which the public sphere would degenerate, 'dominated by the electronic media and pervaded by images and virtual realities. He could scarcely imagine that this milieu of "conversational" enlightenment could be adapted both to non-verbal indoctrination and to deception *by means of* language.'[72]

Nevertheless, Habermas argues, after the terrible events of the twentieth century, the prohibition of war in international law, as a result both of the Kellogg–Briand Pact of 1928 and the Tokyo and Nuremberg military tribunals, does bring us closer to Kant's scheme for perpetual peace. 'With these two innovations, the states as a subject of international law, for the first time, lost the general presumption of innocence of an assumed state of nature.'[73] Moreover, the spread of democracy, increased global economic interconnectedness, and the emergence of a global public sphere based on global media and transnational social movements do seem to suggest that, after all that has been learned from twentieth-century tragedies, the factors which Kant believed would lead to a universal civil society are still in existence.

'Civil society and its rivals'

Wars were between similarly constituted European states. Thus within Europe, civil society was national and contrasted with war in the international arena. Civil societies were also contrasted with uncivil societies, in Eastern Europe and beyond. Thus, if civil society was national within Europe, it was conceived as European outside Europe. On the one hand, civil society was contrasted to the Eastern Empires that ruled on the basis of fear and were sustained by a mixture of physical coercion and superstition. On the other hand, there were societies in North America or Africa, characterized as 'rude', 'savage' or 'barbarian', which were thought to be anarchical.

Most civil society theorists had a teleological view of history; they understood these 'uncivil' societies as backward, less advanced stages in history, which would inevitably lead to civil society – the highest stage mankind had experienced so far. This is a view that even today pervades the thinking of Western donors – the idea that through support for NGOs, the West can help the rest of the world 'catch up'. This conception of civil society has, not surprisingly, given rise to the charge that civil society is a Eurocentric concept, that is to say, a concept born out of the particular cultural context of north-west Europe, not easily transposable to other contexts.

One version of the Eurocentric argument is that put forward by Ernest Gellner. The phrase 'civil society and its rivals' is the subtitle of his book *The Conditions of Liberty* in which he consciously paraphrases Karl Popper's book *The Open Society and its Enemies*. In Gellner's view, civil society is only one possible outcome of modernity – a miraculous outcome achieved by chance in north-western Europe as a result of a compromise between Protestant dissidents and the state. According to Gellner, modernity (science and industrialization) requires what he calls 'modular man'. The term 'modular' is taken from the idea of modular furniture in which components can be fitted together in different ways, while maintaining a harmonious whole. Modular man has certain basic skills, including a shared language, and can adapt himself to a variety of positions in modern society. Modular man takes promises and commitments seriously and is able to enter contracts and associations without rigidity and ritual. Modular man is 'capable of performing highly diverse tasks in the same general cultural idiom, if necessary reading up manuals of specific jobs in the general standard style of the culture in question'.[74] Gellner argues that social contract theories would not have been possible without the emergence of modular man. But while modular man is a necessary condition for civil society, he is by no means a sufficient condition. On the contrary, modular man is vulnerable to collectivist ideologies, especially those based on ethnic identity.

During the twentieth-century, we have witnessed competing models of modern society, based on Gellner's modular man, which could be said to represent the worst fears of thinkers like Ferguson or de Tocqueville. They are coercion-intensive regimes – pacified societies, in which individual freedom is lacking and in which rules are imposed from above rather than through a process of negotiation. In these societies, the distinction between war and peace is less acute since collective forms of social organization predominate. Or to put it another way, in these societies collective organization for war was also the salient element of state-building but, unlike in civil societies, the forms of social organization that predominate in wartime also tend to be sustained in peace-time. Hence, all these societies are governed by collectivist ideologies, which depend on the notion of permanent 'enemies' and potential conflict.

The three main types of collectivist ideologies elaborated by Gellner are nationalism, Islam and Marxism. Nationalism is not necessarily antithetical to civil society; early nineteenth-century European nationalisms or post-colonial nationalisms provided the basis for democracy and state-building. But nationalism also can and often does constitute a vehicle for collectivism, populism and social cohesion in the absence of civil society – a legitimation for dictatorship and war. Islam is, according to Gellner, very similar to nationalism in that it has the capacity to become the 'pervasive membership defining culture of the total society'.[75] Unlike Christianity, however, Islam never generated the kind of Protestant individualism that provided the beginnings of civil society. Islam, according to Gellner, has always been characterized by the distinction between high and low forms of the religion. High Islam is 'scripturalist, rule-oriented, puritanical, liberal, sober, egalitarian, anti-ecstatic'.[76] Low Islam needs priests, mysticism, ritual and living saints. As rural autonomy is destroyed by colonialism, post-colonialism and the various processes of modernity, those people who move from the village to the town aspire to a rule-bound rather than saint-bound form of Islam. Thus 'puritanism and fundamentalism become tokens of urban sophistication'.[77] Unlike Protestantism, Muslim law covers the details of everyday life but not politics. Hence it is ideally suited for 'the long march to a disciplined, modern, industrial society'.[78]

The third 'rival' to civil society is Marxism. Marxism, according to Gellner, was the culmination of enlightenment thought, offering a blueprint not only for political emancipation but for economic emancipation as well. So why did it fail 'so spectacularly'? Part of the answer, given by Gellner, is that the Marxist experiment took place in a society already characterized by tyranny. 'The superimposition of Marxism on Byzantine theology and traditions proved disastrous. Modern administrative and communication technology had made economic centralisation both more feasible and more disastrous than it had been in the days when Russian villages were isolated by impassable mud in spring and autumn and when nature herself, if not human will, had circumscribed autocracy.'[79] But another part of the answer is the totalitarian nature of the ideology itself. Marxism, according to Gellner, sacralized everyday life leaving no room for the profane. The problem was the deification of the present. This explains the contrast between the Stalin era and the Brezhnev era. 'When the *nomenklatura* killed each other and accompanied the murderous rampage with blatantly mendacious political theatre, belief survived; but when the *nomenklatura* switched from shooting each other to bribing each other, faith evaporated. The squalor of the work relationship was the equivalent of corrupt priesthood in other faiths.'[80]

Unlike the classical civil society theorists, Gellner is not a historicist. He argues that these different forms of collectivist ideology are all compatible with the atomism and modularity that characterizes modern society. Moreover, they are all, in a sense, anticipated in the forewarnings of civil society theorists about the danger of passivity and apathy, the tendency to allow material need to take precedence over political freedom, the absence or weakness of active concepts of citizenship. But he does not think that civil society will necessarily win out against its rivals, although the revival of the concept, especially in Eastern Europe, reflects the attractiveness of the civil society model. The revival of the concept, according to Gellner, is an aspiration to gain what has already been achieved in the West, although this may not be achieved. His model of civil society draws heavily on Adam Ferguson, although his definition is more in keeping with contemporary usage, and is inextricably linked to the state. Indeed, he hints that the survival of the state system, now threatened by globalization, may be necessary for the survival of civil society.

An opposite version of the Eurocentric argument, propounded by many third world and left scholars, is that 'uncivil' societies are not simply an alternative route to modernity; rather they are a reaction to European civil society, a consequence of the often violent encounter between European civil society and the rest of the world. The very success of civil society, linked to capitalism, in north-west Europe explains coercion and brutality elsewhere. If European states went to war with each other within Europe, outside Europe they undertook conquest rather than war and the civil society project was European or white rather than national.

The most articulate expression of this argument is expounded by Mahmood Mamdani, in his book *Citizen and Subject: Contemporary Africa and the Legacy of Late Colonialism*.[81] Mamdani argues that civil society (citizenship, rights, and contractual relations) was reserved for whites in the colonial period. The Europeans, in the tradition of stadial history, tended to describe Africans as 'children'; Hegel mythologized Africa as the 'land of childhood'. The colonial state introduced a differentiation between European and 'native' institutions. Europeans enjoyed civic rights and duties, a legal system based on respect for the individual, public debate and association, as well an economic system based on contracts. Among Africans, the Europeans discovered customary, tribal laws that were codified and rigidified by the Europeans; unlike civil law, customary law applied to communities not individuals and was largely based on force. According to Mamdani apartheid was the 'generic form of the colonial state in Africa. As a form of rule, apartheid is what Smuts called institutional segregation, the British termed indirect rule and the French association.'[82] In the post-colonial period, the state was deracialized but the differentiation between 'citizens' among the new national elites in the towns and 'subjects' in the rural areas remained so that the 'tribal logic overwhelmed the democratic logic of civil society . . . This is why civil society politics where the rural is governed through customary law is necessarily patrimonial; urban politicians harness rural-urban constituencies through patron–client relations.' The winner in elections 'is simultaneously the representative power in civil society and the despotic power over Native Authorities'.[83]

A similar argument is put forward by Partha Chatterjee, who argues that in post-colonial societies like India, the domain of civil society – associational life, individual rights, autonomy, deliberation, contract, and so on – is confined to a small post-colonial elite, even though the legal-bureaucratic apparatus extends throughout the population, generally based on force and repression. 'This hiatus is extremely significant because it is the mark of non-western modernity as an always incomplete project of "modernisation" and of the role of an enlightened elite engaged in a pedagogical mission in relation to the rest of society.'[84] Chatterjee proposes that the term 'civil society' should be rejected and replaced by 'political society' (a view which Mamdani shares) where demands can be expressed by the 'subjects' and not just 'citizens' using the language of rights, even if rights apply to collectivities rather than individuals.

Gellner, Mamdani and Chatterjee all share a similar understanding of civil society as a Eurocentric concept, as what the West already has. The difference between them is about whether or not such a concept is a legitimate aspiration or a 'fraud and an illusion' designed to sustain coercive methods of rule. There is an alternative argument that draws on the postmodern version of civil society, which denies the Eurocentric character of civil society and suggests that there was something approximating civil society in other parts of the world, even if there was not the same emphasis on individual autonomy. This argument is particularly important in relation to the Middle East, where it is claimed that Islam is a phenomenon that has to be understood in the context of modernity.[85] It is argued that *Umma* – the concept of Islamic community – was a way of overcoming traditional tribal solidarities not necessarily linked to the state. It was a way of dealing with the anomie associated with an emerging urban and market society. In the most dynamic period of Islamic development, between the seventh and fourteenth centuries, so the argument goes, a sort of civil society existed composed of guilds, associations, bazaars, religious scholars, trusts and foundations, and Sufi orders, that were autonomous from the state and capable of balancing state power. Particularly important was the relationship between *ulama*, religious scholars, and *bazaris*, merchants, producers and shopkeepers. The *bazaris* financed the scholars through *vaqf* (religious endowments), which ensured their independence. The scripturalist approach, described by Gellner, was a kind of public sphere, a way of debating the 'good life' (ethics and morality), for example the meaning of *jihad*. Thus the *munbar* (pulpit) was very important for political debate. Although these organizations were autonomous and self-organized, they were, however, based on communities rather than individuals and membership was ascriptive rather than voluntary. Another Islamic concept, the *bay'a*, through which the ruled express their loyalty to the ruler, is also sometimes likened to a social contract.[86]

There are contemporary versions of this argument to be found among Islamic scholars. Thus Ali Bulac, a Turkish scholar, identifies civil society with Umma and sees the Islamic community as a counter to the state. According to Bulac: 'This modern state developed into a monster which controls all aspects of social and cultural life: law, education, art, religion. It imposes a common nationality on many ethnicities; the logic of the state is ethnic cleansing internally and nationalist wars globally.'[87] The individual has to be freed from the state not as the atom of liberal theory but as part of an Islamic community. Bulac envisages coexisting self-governing religious communities, rather, it seems, on the model of the Ottoman Empire. He cites *Medina Vasikasi*, the charter drawn up by the Prophet to regulate the relations between the new Islamic community and other tribes. This strange mixture of autonomy and tolerance within a communitarian framework also characterizes the current debate about civil society in Iran.[88]

The problem with this postmodern version of civil society, which is to some extent shared in the notions of political society espoused by Mamdani and Chatterjee, is that communitarian traditional associations can be very oppressive. Ernest Gellner is right to insist that individual autonomy and voluntary association constitute the essence of the emancipatory character of civil society. On the other hand, Mamdani and Chatterjee are also right when they argue that the imposition of civil society by colonial states widened the gap between the West and the rest. Indeed, the dynamism of Western Europe during the modern period directly intensified the coercive character of regimes outside the privileged territory of civil society. The second serfdom in Eastern Europe or the spread of slavery in the Americas have to be understood both as a reaction to and a condition for the development of Western Europe. Moreover, this widening gap was increasingly expressed in the discourse of civil society; notions like 'orientalism' were invented to explain the 'backwardness' of other societies.

All the same the argument that civil society was invented in Europe and that its development was associated with conquest, domination and exploitation still does not negate the emancipatory potential of the term. Ideas have no borders and the evolution of human knowledge is characterized by an endless borrowing and mixing of concepts and insights. The revival of the idea of civil society took place not in Western Europe but in Eastern Europe and Latin America where the concepts of individual autonomy and self-organizations offered a new liberating language. The relationship between the actual practice of civil society and coercion elsewhere can be explained, I would argue, not in terms of the ideas themselves but in the territorially bound way in which civil society was realized. Civil society was linked to the war-making colonial state, which constituted a limitation on civil society itself as well as a barrier to the development of civil society elsewhere. Indeed, the new meaning of civil society, which breaks through the territorial boundedness of the concept, has relevance for the West as well as the South.

Reconceptualizing civil society

The revival of the concept of civil society is thus not simply a revival of what went before. And I want to suggest a reformulation of the concept in such a way as to be applicable both to the traditional territorially bound form of civil society and to the new extended aspirations contained in the contemporary concept.

I define civil society as the medium through which one or many social contracts between individuals, both women and men, and the political and economic centres of power are negotiated and reproduced. I use the term social contract both to emphasize an agreed institutional outcome and to reflect the early modernist belief in the role of human reason and will as opposed to either chance or historical determination. But at the same time, I do not mean by a social contract an abstract hypothetical device. Rather, I am referring to a concrete reality. The actual social contract has its defining moments such as the American Declaration of Independence, the Round Tables of 1989 or, in the international arena, the Helsinki Final Act of 1975. But it is also an everyday process of public engagement by self-organized groups and institutions which empower individuals, such as social movements, the media, religious organizations or political parties (sometimes), through which these defining moments are generated and sustained. It is an expression of Tilly's bargaining process but it involves not just bargaining but the existence of a public conversation, a 'good-tempered' conversation. It involves reason and sentiment and not just the conflict of interests and passions. Thus it is not a legalistic type of contract or set of contracts; rather it could perhaps be described as 'politics'.

This definition is compatible with Ernest Gellner's definition that civil society is 'that set of diverse non-governmental institutions, which is strong enough to counterbalance the state and, while not preventing the state from fulfilling its role as keeper of the peace and arbitrator between major interests, can nevertheless prevent it from dominating and atomising the rest of society'.[89] But it goes beyond the definition since it can include efforts to counterbalance the power of transnational or local institutions including both political institutions and large corporations.

It is also close to the definitions both of Arato and Cohen and of John Keane. Thus Arato and Cohen define civil society 'as a sphere of social interaction between economy and state, composed above all of the intimate sphere (especially the family), the sphere of associations (especially voluntary organisations) social movements and forms of public communication'.[90] John Keane uses the term to mean 'a complex and dynamic ensemble of legally protected non-governmental institutions that tend to be non-violent, self-organising, self-reflexive, and permanently in tension with each other and with the state institutions that "frame", construct, and enable their activities'.[91] As is the case with Gellner's definition, both emphasize the relationship to the state rather than to political authority in general and Keane's definition does not refer to the relation to the economy. But beyond that, the terms 'interaction' or 'tension' do not necessarily imply any particular outcome. They do not imply the institutionalization of the content of the contract – the results in terms of legislative action, political culture, policies or actions by states and corporations. A social contract involves interaction but it is more than this; it is purposeful interaction. A social contract also tends to involve tension and even struggle, although this need not necessarily be the case.

This definition of civil society is both an aspiration and a description of a partial and emergent reality. It presupposes that the moral autonomy of individuals does not only imply selfish behaviour and it encompasses the potential for human beings to develop institutions that express universally agreed norms based on actual discursive practice. In other words, the possibilities for extending and enhancing civil society exist but there is no inevitability about the process; it depends on the actions of individuals, acting both together and separately. 'Real' civil society or 'actually existing' civil society is a realm bombarded by images and influences, perpetually 'colonized' both by political salesmanship and consumerist pressures. The end of the Cold War may have freed actually existing civil societies from the superstitions of Cold War ideologies but nevertheless the space for deliberation and discussion is constantly subject to invasion. Thus the term reflects both civil society as it is and the normative aspiration, indeed struggles, for the expansion of unencumbered public space where genuinely free debate and discussion can take place.

It is a rights-based definition of civil society, that is to say, it is about politics from below and about the possibility for human emancipation. Negative liberty is the precondition for a genuine social contract, for 'living in truth', including the liberty not to participate and even to be 'timorous, non-vigilant and absent-minded'. Individuals can choose whether or not to participate in civil society. Nevertheless, a social contract must involve some sort of civic involvement, whether it is the modest virtues of human sympathy and understanding developed through good-tempered conversation or a stronger Tocquevillian form of activism – hence, the definition combines negative and positive liberty. The big question, of course, which forms the basis of much of the rest of this book is whether this is enough – whether reason and moral sentiment and/or civic activism can provide the basis for social solidarity in place of external conflict or collectivist identities.

Up to now, the social contract has been primarily defined in relation to the territorially defined state although it has taken different forms as the state has passed through various stages, from constitutional monarchies to the modern nation-state to the warfare/welfare states of the twentieth century, reflecting the changing nature of the contract. It is true that, for the territorial state, war played an important role in determining the shape of the social contract, although compromises reached in war almost always reflected demands and proposals that had been put forward in peacetime in public debate and discussion. Indeed, the ability to win a series of wars, which established both the reality and the legitimacy of the state, in part depended on the internal possibilities for compromise. Moreover, extensions of rights and increased emancipation was not always achieved through war, especially in smaller states where civil society has been more active and public debate more intense and extensive.

The social contract associated with the construction of the state could be said to have taken the form of Tilly's bargain; civil and political rights were guaranteed in exchange for paying taxes and fighting in wars. The individual rights that citizens enjoyed in peacetime were exchanged for the abrogation of those rights in wartime. In wartime, the citizens became part of a collectivity, the nation, and had to be ready to die for the state.

In exchange for civil and political rights in peacetime, the individual citizen accepted a kind of unlimited liability in wartime. Of course, both rights and liabilities have expanded over time. As war shifted from the limited professional wars of the eighteenth century, through the conscript citizen wars of the nineteenth century to the total wars of the twentieth century where every single person was vulnerable, so it is possible to see an extension first of civil and political rights in the nineteenth century and then economic and social rights in the twentieth century. Moreover, this evolution is not only to be explained in terms of the bargain between the two developments. Each had their own logic: the Western Way of War tended to extremes, as Clausewitz pointed out; and the extension of civil rights set in motion demands for political and, later, economic and social rights, as T. H. Marshall has made clear.[92] At the same time, however, the growth of surveillance, the wartime atmosphere, the national security apparatus have increasingly constituted an infringement of rights, albeit partial and/or temporary. Indeed war and the rhetoric of war could be represented as a mechanism for suppressing civil society.[93]

Nor was it just war which restricted the concept of civil society. The existence of coercive regimes in other parts of the world and the participation in conquest and colonization represented a denial of the assumption of human equality on which the concept of civil society was originally based. The stadial view of history gave rise to a view of other peoples as not quite human – children or savages – and this permitted a scale of brutality totally at variance with Ferguson's notions of 'civilized' warfare. The existence, moreover, of 'uncivil' societies provided a kind of excuse for the imperfections of actually existing civil societies. 'Why not demonstrate in Moscow?' seemed a convincing retort to those who protested against the Cold War.

How does this definition relate to the ambiguities of meanings in the concept of civil society? My argument is that both the changing content of civil society and the changing character of political authority reflect the terms of the social contract in different periods. In the seventeenth and early eighteenth centuries, when the central demand was for a rule-governed society, which guaranteed private security, civil society was coterminous with the state and distinct from the non-civil societies – empires or anarchy. As demands were extended to cover political rights, the accountability of government to citizens, so civil society became distinct from the state and was identified with the new capitalist class who were demanding access to political decision-making. In the twentieth century, when demands were further extended to economic and social rights, civil society was redefined to exclude the private sector as well. It was the new workers' movements who became the main constituents of civil society. In the twenty-first century, as I shall argue in the next chapter, the content has changed again. Civil society has become transnational. It remains distinct from profit organizations unless they provide a medium for public pressure but its focus is public affairs not the market. Likewise it is distinct from the state although it might include state-funded organizations if they are capable of acting in a genuinely autonomous manner. Unlike earlier definitions, the family is not excluded since what were formerly considered private issues – women's rights, rights of sexual minorities, domestic violence – have become a part of the public debate.

Up to the twenty-first century, however, the territorial bound-edness of actually existing civil society, the link with the war-making colonial state, constituted a fundamental limitation on the reach of civil society. The revival of civil society in the 1970s and 1980s has to be understood, first and foremost, as a reaction to those fundamental limitations posed by war and colonialism or by societies organized for war. How this came about and what it entails is the subject of the next chapter.

3
The Ideas of 1989: The Origins of the Concept of Global Civil Society

'With all the fuss and noise,' wrote François Furet, the French historian, 'not a single new idea has come out of Eastern Europe in 1989.'[1] Timothy Garton Ash, in his eyewitness account of the 1989 revolutions, said much the same thing. 'The ideas whose time has come are old, familiar ones. (It is the new ideas whose time has passed.)'[2] And Jürgen Habermas noted 'a peculiar characteristic of this revolution, namely its total lack of ideas that are either innovative or oriented towards the future'.[3] He described the 1989 revolutions as 'nachholende revolutionen' ('rectifying revolutions' or 'revolutions of recuperation').[4]

It is true that the revolutionaries of 1989 did not propose new policies or strategies for governments or even new forms of government (and in the last two hundred years, competing ideas have tended to focus on what states ought to be doing). But the period of the 1980s, which preceded the revolutions, was a ferment of ideas to which social movements in both East and West contributed. These ideas centred on the coming together of peace and human rights, on a new understanding of citizenship and civil society, and on transnationalism or internationalism at the level of society. The notion of European or global civil society, which could be said to have emerged during this period, can be said in some sense to encompass or encapsulate these strands of thinking.

It is worth noting that in the postscript to the new tenth-anniversary edition of his book *We the People*, Timothy Garton Ash somewhat revises his opinion about whether there were new ideas. What was new, he now says, was the method – the non-violence, the self-organization, the readiness to compromise – the 'how' not the 'what' of the revolution.[5] But, as I shall argue, the 'how' is a crucial component of new ways of thinking about politics in the contemporary situation.

This chapter is about the emergence of the new ideas, what they meant at the time and why they were new. It is about how the groups and individuals who opposed the Cold War rediscovered the concepts described in the previous chapter and gave them new contemporary interpretations – interpretations which were to resonate in the new global configuration on the twenty-first century. The main part of the chapter describes what happened in the 1980s from the perspective of what were then called new social movements in West and Central Europe and the evolution of ideas. The last part draws out the conceptual implications of the ideas and their relation to the meanings of civil society elaborated in the previous chapter.

It is worth noting at the outset that this was not a purely European phenomenon; similar ideas and practices were being developed elsewhere, particularly in Latin America. Rather, the language developed by the East Europeans and the inspiration of the 1989 revolutions offered a way to express and even legitimize what was happening in other parts of the world.

The 1980s

I want to start with two preliminary general remarks. First of all, in most accounts of the 1989 revolutions, rather little attention is paid to agency. Most explanations focus on the economic and moral bankruptcy of the communist regimes and the coming to power of Gorbachev; sometimes the effect of Reagan's nuclear policies is also included as an explanation. Undoubtedly, these factors were important. But the first factor – the economic situation – is insufficient as an explanation; it explains the context but not why the revolutions happened. And while the role of individuals in history can be important, no single individual can bear the weight of the 1989 revolutions. So this chapter focuses on agency – the actions and behaviour and thinking of the actors who actually carried out the revolutions in the period immediately preceding 1989.

A second general remark concerns the coming together of peace and human rights, which, as will be explained, was an important precondition for the notion of global civil society. During the Cold War, these concepts were strictly separated and indeed their separation can be said to have reflected the continuing salience of the Great Divide as it applied in a Cold War context. Peace was about relations between collectivities, i.e. states, and referred to the international arena; human rights were about the universal rights of individuals but were put into practice within the territorial boundaries of the state. Thus 'peace' was a word espoused by the Soviet Union, reflecting its collectivist ideology centred around the notion of permanent struggle, which was built on the terrible experiences of the Second World War. 'Peace' was a justification for the Soviet war system in the face of what was promulgated as Western aggression and, also for pragmatic reasons, a way to maintain the status quo in Europe and 'catch up' in the arms race. As Václav Havel pointed out in an essay addressed to the West European peace movement 'An Anatomy of Reticence', the word 'peace' had thus been stripped of all its content.[6] As a consequence, those who opposed the Cold War and nuclear weapons in the West and who described their organizations as peace movements gave the appearance of being apologists for the Soviet system, albeit unwittingly. It was therefore relatively easy to marginalize their activities.

The West espoused 'human rights' and, for many on the left, this phrase was also discredited partly because some distrusted the liberal individualistic assumptions underlying human rights which did not fit with their communitarian vision, and, more importantly, because of the instrumental way in which the term was used. The popularity of human rights as an expression of struggle had emerged out of the anti-colonial struggles as well as the civil liberties movements in the USA. Human rights issues were taken up by the Carter Administration in the mid-1970s. It was only later that post-Carter Administrations began to use the term more cynically as a tool in the Cold War. Human rights violations in places like Pakistan or Brazil under military rule or Pinochet's Chile were ignored because these regimes were anti-communist, part of the 'Free World'. Hence, many peace activists understood human rights merely as Cold War rhetoric. It was the breakdown of the separation between peace and human rights – first from above, in the 1975 Helsinki Accord, and then from below as opposition groups in East and West embraced each other's causes – which contributed in important ways to the 1989 revolutions and the end of the Cold War.

Ideas in East Central Europe

The main sources of new ideas were the intellectuals in Central Europe in the late 1970s and 1980s. During the 1950s and 1960s, the main form of opposition was reform communism or revisionism. Thinkers like György Lukacs or Leszek Kolakowski, who were to influence the 1968 generation, outlined the possibilities for a human socialism, while remaining firmly within the Marxist tradition. Revisionism was defeated first in 1953 (East Germany), then in 1956 (Hungary and Poland), and finally in 1968 (Czechoslovakia). The Soviet invasion of Czechoslovakia dealt a death blow to the hopes of reforming communism. It was an 'existential shock', the East German writer Christa Wolf was later to say.[7] And Kolakowski wrote that communism 'ceased to be an intellectual problem, and became merely a question of power'.[8]

After 1968, the main form of opposition was the individual dissident. The dissidents saw themselves not as precursors of a political movement but as individuals who wanted to retain their personal integrity. Dissidence was about the dignity of the individual as much as about politics. It was about the possibility of honest interaction even at a private and personal level, about being able to read, think and discuss freely. Jacek Kuroń, one of the key democratic thinkers in Poland, explains that the idea of self-organization began long before the formation of Solidarity. 'We started many, many years before. Recalling those years, in light of what has now been accomplished, I look back in astonishment. It was so simple then. What we wanted was to read books, talk to each other freely, to collect money for people needing help: the simplest human actions. Yet one can organize society around these simple actions and goals, and this very fact is like a time bomb ticking away under totalitarianism.'[9] George Konrad, the Hungarian writer, talked about 'networks of sympathy'.[10] It was in these networks that the new ideas originated.

A turning point was the 1975 Helsinki Accord. This was the high point of a new détente between East and West and it expressed, perhaps for the first time, the erosion of the Great Divide, the commitment to both peace and human rights within a single document. The Helsinki Accord, on the one hand, confirmed the territorial status quo in Europe, for which the Soviet Union had pressed, and, on the other hand, contained commitments to respect human rights, which the East Europeans had accepted under Western pressure. The initial reaction in East European opposition circles was negative. Western leaders were to be seen embracing Soviet leaders and the commitment to human rights was thought to be purely cosmetic. At first sight, this was just a renewed Concert of Europe, a way in which the Great Powers reached agreement from above without taking into consideration the concerns of ordinary people. After all, when Nixon and Kissinger went to Moscow in 1972, they ignored the Jewish refuseniks protesting at the gates of the Kremlin. According to Milan Šimecka, who was later to become a Charter 77 spokesperson:

> I remember how all those disarmament talks in the seventies – even Helsinki itself – looked very dubious dealing to us, like a party at the expense of the East Europeans which we paid for in the currency of imprisonment, decline, and stagnation. This was not entirely true, of course, and as it turned out, what seemed no more than agreements on paper about human rights were, amazingly enough, to prove instrumental in achieving certain improvements. The third basket at Helsinki was originally intended as the price the Soviet Union had to pay for recognition of the status quo in Europe. The Soviet Union was only too happy to pay it, since our political culture contained thousands of artfully contrived methods for skirting human rights obligations. Indeed, in Czechoslovakia, the immediate post-Helsinki period was a time of the worst persecutions. A deaf ear was turned to any reference to the Helsinki Final Act and, as I know from personal experience, any talk of Helsinki in those days would send police officers into fits of laughter.
>
> That all assumes a different aspect, however, if looked at in longer perspective. Over these past years . . . much has changed. Concepts have emerged which were previously unknown. These concepts undoubtedly penetrated the reform thinking then coming to fruition in the Soviet Union. If nothing else, by confirming the outcome of World War II, Helsinki served to rid the Soviet Union of its old

obsessions about external threats, and this subsequently had a positive effect on its attitude to détente.[11]

A similar point was made by Adam Michnik:

On the other hand, it was the time of Détente, the time of the
Helsinki Agreement, part of which was a so called third basket – a
basket of human rights. And this basket, which in the eyes of our
Communist leaders was just a decoration without any importance,
became for us, opposition people, an instrument in trying to loosen
the tight corset of Communist dictatorship. What used to be closely
guarded internal matters of every Communist regime became a
subject of international monitoring, and international institutions –
like the Helsinki Watch, which were then created, and gained huge
importance monitoring repression of human rights in Communist
countries.[12]

In the late 1970s, Helsinki provided the impetus for the formation
of new groups to defend human rights – Charter 77 in Czechoslovakia, KOR (the defence of workers) in Poland and the Democratic Opposition in Hungary. It was during this period that
the new ideas began to emerge. A key text was Adam Michnik's
path-breaking essay 'The New Evolutionism' written in 1978.[13]
Michnik argues that the task of the opposition was not to seize
power but to change the relationship between state and society.
Through self-organization, it was possible to create autonomous
spaces in society up to the limits imposed by the Brezhnev Doctrine, i.e. the threat of Soviet intervention. It was Michnik who
rediscovered the term civil society.[14] But he used it in a new way,
not merely as the rule of law and the institutions to check abuses
of the state, but the emphasis was on self-organization, autonomy,
solidarity and non-violence. Of course, nothing is really new –
Michnik's concept of civil society was probably closest to that of
de Tocqueville. Nevertheless in the context of the overbearing
state and the emergence of new groups and movements, the term
had an entirely new resonance, as a political aspiration and tech-
nique and not just an analytical tool.

Similar concepts were developed elsewhere in Central Europe.
These included: 'Anti-Politics'[15] (the term developed by Václav
Havel and George Konrad) – a sphere of society that escapes the
total hold of the overbearing state; 'Living in Truth' (Václav

Havel) – the notion of refusing the lies of the political class; or the 'parallel *polis*' developed in Czechoslovakia – the idea of an Aristotelian *polis* organized around the good life, which would, as it were, spread out and gradually chip away at the formal political institutions. In 'The Power of the Powerless' Havel described the grocer who puts the slogan 'Workers of the World Unite' in his shop window not because he believes it but as a badge of loyalty.[16] Milan Kusý, another Czechoslovak intellectual, talked about the 'as if game' in which the grocer behaves 'as if' he believes in the slogan and the authorities behave 'as if' they believe he believes.[17] This is a system in which every individual is both victim and accomplice. The realm of 'anti-politics' or the parallel *polis* was one where the individual would refuse such collaboration with the regime, however token, in which the 'as if game' would be rejected. In all these discussions, the role of the individual and the importance of personal links, something that was central to individual dissidence, were considered primary, overriding claims to political authority.

The Chartists saw themselves as developing a 'new type of politics, or rather a revival of what was once understood by the term "politics", the way it was practised, and which has, today, been almost forgotten'.[18] According to Václav Benda, the parallel *polis* 'does not compete for power. Its aim is not to replace the power of another kind, but rather under this power – or beside it – to create a structure that represents other laws and in which the voice of the ruling power is heard only as an insignificant echo from a world that is organised in an entirely different way.'[19] They described themselves not as a movement but as a civic initiative, a 'small island in a sea of apathy'.[20] For George Konrad and the Hungarian democratic opposition, anti-politics was about pushing the state out of everyday life. It was a new type of politics because it was not about the capture of state power; it was the politics 'of those who don't want to be politicians and don't want to share power. Anti-politics is the emergence of forums that can be appealed to against political power; it is a counter power that cannot take power and does not wish to. Power it has already, here and now, by reason of its moral and cultural weight.'[21]

The proponents of these new concepts did not regard them as only relevant to communist or authoritarian societies. On the contrary, they believed that their situation was only one symptom of a broader crisis, which Havel described as the 'global technological civilisation' and Konrad related to the arms race and the threat of nuclear war. (The term 'globalization' is explicitly used in Konrad's book *Anti-Politics*.) Indeed, they argued that, without the partial illusion of democratic freedoms, they were able to see the situation more clearly. Havel wrote:

> The post-totalitarian system is only one aspect – a particularly drastic aspect and thus all the more revealing of its real origins – of the general inability of modern humanity to be master of its own situation. The automatism of the post-totalitarian system is merely an extreme version of the global automatism of technological civilisation. The human failure that it mirrors is only one variant of the general failure of humanity. . . . It would appear that the traditional parliamentary democracies can offer no fundamental opposition to the automatism of technological civilisation and the industrial-consumer society, for they, too, are being dragged helplessly along. People are manipulated in ways that are infinitely more subtle and refined than the brutal methods used in post-totalitarian societies. . . . In a democracy, human beings may enjoy many personal freedoms and securities that are unknown to us, but in the end they do them no good, for they too are ultimately victims of the same automatism, and are incapable of defending their concerns about their own identity or preventing their superficialisation or transcending concerns about their own personal survival to become proud and responsible members of the *polis*, making a genuine contribution to the creation of its destiny.[22]

For Konrad, the issue was global militarization and the risk of a 'global Auschwitz'. He was concerned not just about Central Europe but the dangers to the world that arise from the awesome power accumulated by modern leaders. 'The Soviet and American Presidents have more power than all the tyrants of history combined . . . I look at those two faces and I blanch. I wouldn't entrust the fate of humanity to even Aristotle and Kant.'[23] Thus anti-politics is not just about changing Central Europe; it is about changing the world. 'Anti-politics offers a radical alternative to the philosophy of a nuclear *ultima ratio*. Anti-politics strives to put politics in its place and make sure it stays there, never overstepping its proper office of defending and refining the rules of the game of civil society. Anti-politics is the ethos of civil society, and civil society is the antithesis of military society. There are more or less militarised societies – societies under the sway of nation-states whose officials consider total war one of the possible moves in the game. Thus, military society is the reality, civil society is the utopia.'[24]

Konrad also made it clear that the Central European idea of democracy was not simply to copy the democracy of the West; of course, they wanted parliamentary democracy, but they also wanted democracy in the workplace and among local communities 'especially in those areas where we meet face to face and can look in the eye the people who make decisions in our name and ask us to carry them out'.[25]

All the Central European thinkers emphasized what was known as the 'return to Europe' – the idea that the Cold War division must be overcome and the terms of the Yalta agreement in 1945 must be opposed (the agreement in 1945 to carve up Europe among Western and Soviet spheres of influence, 'that dirty trick of history' as Konrad called it). This is the thrust of the Prague Appeal addressed to the European peace movements in 1985, which called for the withdrawal of Soviet and American troops from Europe and the reunification of Germany.

The implication of the argument about the global applicability of the ideas of anti-politics, parallel *polis* or civil society, is that what is needed is not just a Central European movement but a 'dialogue high above the level of governments and national boundaries'.[26] Konrad talked about the 'world marketplace of ideas', the need for an 'international public sphere...(which can) curb the tendency of the state to be omnipresent'.[27] He referred to the 'existence of a world forum (which) favours the emergence of the eccentric, of those who stand out...The international alliance of dissenters and avant-gardists takes under its wing those few people who, in their various ways, think their thoughts through to the end.'[28]

These ideas reflected a new reality in Central Europe – the emergence of social movements and citizens' groups, often with trans-European and even global links. The best known was Solidarity in Poland but there was also Swords into Ploughshares in the GDR and the Dialogue Group, a young people's peace group, in Hungary. The New Cold War of the early 1980s squeezed the space for these groups. The crackdown on Solidarity took place in 1981. And the deployment of cruise missiles and a new generation of Soviet missiles provided the occasion for the authorities to try to disperse Swords into Ploughshares and the Dialogue Group.

In the late 1980s, a second generation of groups and movements developed. These included Frieden und Menschenrechtung (Peace and Human Rights) in the GDR led by Bärbel Bohley, Wolnosc i Pokoj (Freedom and Peace) in Poland, several small peace groups in Czechoslovakia such as the Independent Peace Association or the John Lennon Society, and the Danube Circle and FIDESZ (the young democrats) in Hungary. The spread of these groups, however small, began to undermine the sustainability of the regimes, which depended on total control – small autonomous spaces were multiplying. And it was these groups who helped to organize the mass demonstrations and who participated, along with the earlier generation, in the Round Table talks.

Ideas among the West European peace movements

A second source of new ideas was the West European peace movement which exploded across Western Europe in the early 1980s in response to the Nato decision to deploy a new generation of nuclear weapons in Europe – cruise and Pershing missiles. The peace movement has to be understood as the outgrowth or even culmination of the 'new' social movements that developed in Western Europe after 1968. Indeed, many of the activists of the 1980s in both East and West shared a common heritage in having lived through or having even been involved in the 1968 events. Many of the ideas of that period, the reaction to the overbearing and paternalistic state, the emphasis on the radicalization of democracy, the notion of the public sphere, and also the ideas of the feminist movement about changing power relations, were to inform the thinking of the peace movements. Moreover, the peace movement had its own legacy in the anti-nuclear movements of the late 1950s and 1960s and the anti-Vietnam War movement.

In a way, the peace movement can also be considered an offshoot of the Helsinki process, even though peace activists were less aware than their Central European counterparts of the content of the Helsinki Accords. In the atmosphere of détente that followed the Helsinki Accords, the fading of the Soviet threat and the increased travel and communication with the East, it seemed unthinkable to deploy a new generation of nuclear weapons in Europe and to return to the hostile rhetoric of the 1950s. There were peace camps at all the proposed missile bases – Greenham Common being the most well known – and some 5 million people demonstrated against the missiles across Europe in the autumn of 1981 and again in the autumn of 1983.

Parts of the new peace movement – most notably European Nuclear Disarmament (END) led by the historian E. P. Thompson, the Dutch Inter-Church Peace Council whose Secretary General was Mient Jan Faber, and the West German Greens whose most well-known spokesperson was Petra Kelly – put the emphasis on opposition to the Cold War and not just nuclear weapons. END called for a transcontinental movement of citizens and made an explicit link between peace and democracy or human rights. Echoes of Central European ideas can be found in the thinking of the peace movements, although the discourse was less elaborated. The issue of nuclear weapons was treated as a democracy issue. How can we claim to be democratic when control over life and death is in the hands not even of our own politicians but decided in Washington or Brussels? How can nuclear weapons be used to defend human rights when their use would kill millions of people? Getting rid of nuclear weapons was to be achieved, not by seizing power but as in the East, by changing the relations between state and society. Some of the ideas developed in the women's movement during the 1970s had relevance to this kind of politics; the term 'control over our lives' rearticulated the feminist concern with 'control over our bodies'. Nuclear weapons and the apparatus around them were seen as a 'male' totalitarian enclave in our society. The mantra 'deterrence keeps the peace' could be viewed, at least for powerholders, as the Western equivalent of 'Workers of the World Unite'.

The concept of 'defensive defence' or 'defensive deterrence' expressed the notion that defence is much more effective than offence in an era of highly accurate destructive capacity; a strategy that eschews military offensive capabilities, especially nuclear weapons, can both deter an enemy attack by threatening to inflict high attrition rates, and, at the same time, open up the possibility for greater cooperation by removing the threat that its offensive capabilities pose. This concept was translated by the Soviet New Thinkers into 'reasonable sufficiency' and allowed big reductions in tanks, missiles and aircraft.[29] The idea of 'common security', developed by doyens of the détente period such as Olof Palme and Egon Bahr, was that in an era of mutual vulnerability, nuclear overkill had no possible military rationale and, indeed, military power was no longer an effective way to pursue political goals;[30] this idea provided the impetus for Gorbachev's 'Our Common European Home'. Finally, 'human security' referred to the link between peace and human rights, that it is the individual's security that matters not the security of the state. The Helsinki agreement and its progeny, the CSCE (Conference on Security and Cooperation in Europe) process, was viewed as a model for a new approach to security issues, which combined agreements about non-aggression with commitments to individual rights and to cooperation. The idea of reuniting Europe as a way of ending war echoed the East European preoccupation with the 'Return to Europe'.[31]

These proposals for new security approaches by states were paralleled by a new emphasis on the transnational role of citizens. E. P. Thompson talked about a 'healing process' between East and West, about creating autonomous spaces beneath the structures of the Cold War through which citizens could come together. Mient Jan Faber coined the phrase 'détente from below' to complement the détente from above initiated by the Helsinki process. As in the East, a similar emphasis was placed on personal relations. The END Appeal of 1980, largely drafted by E. P. Thompson, stated:

> We must defend and extend the right of all citizens, East and West, to take part in this common movement and to engage in every kind of exchange . . . We must commence to act as if [was this a conscious reference to the 'as if' game?] a united, neutral, pacific Europe already exists. We must learn to be loyal not to 'East' or 'West' but to each other and must disregard the prohibitions and limitations imposed by any national state.[32]

What the new peace movement did was to try to put 'peace' and 'freedom' together again, as E. P. Thompson put it. Both blocs were viewed as restricting the freedom of their citizens. The ideology of deterrence was a form of discipline – an ever-present external threat that maintained cohesion. Underlying this approach was a different analysis of the Cold War. Both left and right had conceived the Cold War as a conflict of systems. For the right, it was a conflict between freedom and totalitarianism; hence anyone who supported the West was 'free' – even patently undemocratic states like Turkey or Brazil. For the left, it was a conflict between capitalism and socialism; hence the reluctance of many

on the left who considered themselves to be committed socialists
to condemn the Soviet Union. The new argument held that the
Cold War was a 'virtual conflict', a 'joint venture', which both
sides needed to sustain their military institutions and their spheres
of influence.[33] It had an 'inertial logic' – a mutually reinforcing
system of 'exterminism'.[34] It was not necessarily a symmetric joint
venture; indeed Migone echoed Gramsci in contrasting the hegemony of the United States, based on the consent of Western
Europe, with the domination of the Soviet Union in Eastern
Europe, based on coercion.[35] But it was a system in which the
two sides fed off each other. The détente period had led to
increasing diversity within the blocs. In Eastern Europe, new
forms of pluralism had begun to develop, including the Polish
workers' movement Solidarity. At the same time, Western
Europe was drifting away from the United States. The so-called
New Cold War of the early 1980s was a way of reimposing
cohesion. In cracking down on Solidarity in December 1981, for
example, the Polish and Soviet governments used the security
argument to justify their actions. This thinking was close to
many of the East European intellectuals, particularly George
Konrad in Hungary and Jaroslav Šabata in Czechoslovakia. 'Anyone who believes that the two systems are pitted against each
other today,' wrote Konrad, 'has fallen victim to the secularised
metaphysics of our civilisation, which looks for a duel between
God and Satan in what is, after all, only a game.'[36]

The appeal for a nuclear-free Europe from Poland to Portugal,
rather than the Atlantic to the Urals as some proposed, emphasized
the political character of the appeal, the need to free Europe from
the post-war 'occupation' by the United States and the Soviet
Union. As Thompson put it in an interview with the Soviet dissident Roy Medvedev, who had signed the Appeal: 'One reason for
the failure of past movements for peace and democracy is that they
have been isolated as "pro-American" or "pro-Soviet" – that is,
serving the advantage of one or other bloc. END intends to break
down this constriction by promoting exchanges between citizens
without the mediation of the official or quasi-official representatives of States, Parties, etc. – that is, by promoting honest communication and discussion of differences, exchanging proposals with
each other.'[37]

The Appeal was signed by thousands of people including prominent names like Olof Palme, Michael Foot, Václav Havel, Roy

Medvedev and others. Nevertheless, END did not represent the peace movement. There were many groups and individuals who still argued that it was important to give priority to opposition to Western nuclear weapons, that talk of democracy and human rights played to the rhetoric of the Cold warriors, that links with dissidents were dangerous and could undermine progress in disarmament. Thus the END position was bitterly contested. In particular, the annual END conventions, which brought together activists from all over Europe, were the sites of divisive debates about whether or not to invite official peace committees. These debates can be seen, however, as a form of education. The new younger generation, who were able to travel to Eastern Europe more easily, were less influenced by past ideologies and learned about the character of the Cold War relatively free from the prejudices of traditional left–right struggles.

The importance of the dialogue

The dialogue between these movements was initiated by those parts of the Western peace movement (most notably END, the Inter-Church Peace Council (IKV) in the Netherlands and the Greens in West Germany) that put the emphasis on opposition to the Cold War. Initially, the concern was partly tactical, to demonstrate in practice that concerns about nuclear war were genuine and not manipulated by the Kremlin. In Poland, where Solidarity had received enormous public support from Western governments, it was, at first, difficult to find common ground. In East Germany and Hungary, the anti-nuclear movements quickly found partners with whom to exchange ideas and projects. In East Germany, a mass movement rapidly developed under the auspices of the Protestant Church, known as 'Swords into Ploughshares'. And in Czechoslovakia, an important dialogue between the peace movement and Charter 77 began with an exchange of letters between E. P. Thompson and Jaroslav Šabata and culminated with the Prague Appeal addressed to the West European peace movements in 1985, which called for the removal of foreign troops and nuclear weapons from the continent of Europe.

From 1980 onwards, the East and West German Churches held an annual peace week. And in 1982, a peace forum on the anniversary of the bombing of Dresden drew some 5,000 young people.

The main issues were conscription and the right to conscientious objection and militarism in schools. An active women's peace movement developed after the East German state tried to introduce conscription for women. The role of writers like Christa Wolf or Stefan Heym was very important, as was the role of Robert Havermann, the Marxist dissident and well-known physicist. Support from the Churches in West Germany and the Netherlands was very important in sustaining the movement, as was the influence of the West European peace movement.

In Hungary, the Dialogue Group developed among young people in the early 1980s through cooperation with END. For these young people, the crucial demand was dialogue. They wanted to be able to demonstrate like Western young people. They wanted to be able to travel freely. The support from END was crucial, not only in practical terms like making the badges, which showed clasped hands holding a flower in the shape of a peace symbol in the Hungarian colours, and in publicizing the group, but more importantly, as became clear later, in providing political space. The Dialogue Group was tolerated by the authorities because of the argument, explicitly put to them by END visitors to Budapest, that the existence of an independent campaign in Hungary would help the campaign against cruise missiles; it would be a way of answering the jibe 'why not demonstrate in Moscow?' At its height, the Dialogue badges could be seen all over Budapest and the Dialogue Group was allowed to demonstrate against nuclear weapons and to organize an East–West peace camp.

After the deployment of the missiles in 1983, there was a crackdown on both the East German and Hungarian movements. The East German crackdown was more severe; several activists were arrested and forced to leave East Germany. But pressure on the young people in Hungary led to the dissolution and split-up of the Dialogue Group. After the deployment of cruise missiles in 1983, the major thrust of parts of the Western peace movement like END, IKV and the Greens was the process of 'détente from below'. Hundreds of activists travelled to Eastern Europe and identified local groups, individuals, town councils and churches, with whom they could talk and exchange ideas. I have before me as I write a leaflet published by END called 'Go East':

> Forget smoke-filled rooms, this political organisation is asking you
> to take a holiday – in Eastern Europe. The Cold War is strictly for

'50s spy thrillers and Levy ads. The peoples of Europe should be friends. Especially young people – we didn't make the division of Europe and we don't have to accept it. Simply by going East, you can start to break down the barriers that split our continent...

The late 1980s was a period of intense communications. A European network for East–West Dialogue was established involving representatives from all the groups in Eastern Europe. In Poland, a new young people's movement began called Freedom and Peace, strongly influenced in its tactics by the Western peace movement and supported by END and the European network. They began as a protest against the oath of loyalty that conscripts have to make to the Warsaw Pact. They strongly believed in non-violence and claimed that the non-violence of Solidarity was not serious since it did not extend to opposition to the arms race. These young people influenced the attitudes of Solidarity leaders. As Adam Michnik put it, in an interview in 1988:

> Just like in the West, new movements and new phenomena are being born here which no-one in their right mind can ignore. Whatever one might think about them – movements like the Greens in the German Federal Republic or the peace movements in Great Britain – one cannot deny their existence because they are an important new element in the political map ... One has to say that it is the Greens and those peace movements who are looking for allies here in movements such as Wolnosc i Pokoj and that is something invaluable. This is extremely significant particularly as it forms part of the peace-making process. It is typical of the Russians that they want to talk about reducing the number of missiles but they don't want to talk about the civil right to refuse to do military service as a way of guaranteeing peace. Why do they not want to talk about this? This is the great merit of these movements at least here in Poland (and, I think, also in the West) – that the problem of war and the army has been interpreted as a problem concerning human rights. Furthermore, when people ask me what I think about the Western peace movements, I always answer with another question: What do those movements think of Yalta? If those movements are for a unified democratic Europe, and if they are struggling for this unity without resorting to violence, then I am for them. I am for them because I believe that there lies the future.[38]

The same year, Jacek Kuroń, one of the key intellectuals in Solidarity, and Janusz Onyskiewicz, the spokesman of Solidarity, attended the END Convention in Lund. E. P. Thompson and Jacek Kuroń publicly embraced in a church in Lund symbolizing the reunion of 'peace' and 'freedom'.

In Czechoslovakia, a similar young people's group was formed called the Independent Peace Association. The Czech jazz section had been one of the earliest signatories of the END Appeal and, in the late 1980s, John Lennon became one of the symbols of the young peace movement. And in Hungary, a new dialogue group was formed known as the West–East Dialogue Group. This group later renamed themselves as the Young Democrats (FIDESZ) and became for some years the ruling party in Hungary, although their character has changed substantially.[39]

A series of East–West seminars was organized in the late 1980s in Poland, Czechoslovakia and Hungary. In Hungary, the seminar held in a music school (the place being kept a secret until the very last minute) was the first legal public event of its kind. In Poland, the meeting was held in a church and several Westerners were refused visas even though they only applied for tourist visas. And in Czechoslovakia, everyone was arrested and the foreigners thrown out of the country. They were accused of being 'NATO agents posing as tourists'!

The dialogue between the peace movement and the East European groups was important in several respects. First of all, the East–West strategy was by no means widely accepted. On the contrary, it was bitterly contested within the peace movement, among the Central European groups and in the dialogue between them. The decade of the 1980s was a period of intense debate about how to achieve democracy and human rights in Eastern Europe. Which came first, peace or democracy? What was the appropriate strategy for ending the Cold War? There were those in the peace movement who argued that human rights would follow disarmament and that the worst evil was nuclear weapons; by taking up the human rights issue, groups like END were endorsing the Western leaders' Cold War rhetoric and thus redu-cing the chances of disarmament. And there were those in the East who argued that the Soviet Union only understands force and the West therefore needed to be strong; unilateralism was appea-sement and disarmament would only be possible after the fall of communism

There was also intense debate about how to relate to dictators and oppressors. At one end of the scale, there were those, primarily in Communist Parties but also the German Social Democrats, who considered that the priority was a dialogue with officials, particularly the peace committees, and that dialogue with the opposition should not publicly disturb this official dialogue. And at the other end of the scale, there were those, primarily in the opposition in the East, who felt there should be no communication with officials, that any communication was a form of collaboration. In between there was a range of positions, which varied according to particular situations.

These debates were a form of education, a learning process. The thinking of many individuals was profoundly influenced by these discussions. By the end of the decade there was a growing consensus, at least among those who took part in the dialogue, that democracy in Eastern Europe was the best strategy for ending the Cold War but, at the same time, democracy could be best achieved within the framework of a détente process and a wind down of the arms race. Moreover, this common understanding was based on changed meanings of both democracy and the international framework. Democracy was not just liberal democracy; it also had to be complemented by a more radical and substantial concept of participation and active citizenship. In an Open Letter to the British peace movements, Charter 77 explained this perspective:

> Your 'sideways' stand, as it were, in relation to the classical democratic structures and political mechanism is very close to the sense and forms of our own efforts. Here again, we must stress, however, our deep conviction that these structures constitute a vital basis which has been denied or falsified always at the cost of greater evil; but at the same time we are aware that the decline of those structures has done much to create the present global crisis, and that without radical new impulses and regenerating transformations no way out of the crisis can be found.[40]

And détente was not just a phenomenon between states; it required a common monitoring by citizens in both halves of Europe. Havel, who was a signatory of the 1980 END Appeal, echoed its sentiments when he wrote, in his address to the European peace movements in 1985:

> It seems to be that all of us, East and West, face one fundamental task from which all else will follow. That task is one of resisting

vigilantly, thoughtfully, and attentively, but at the same time with total dedication, at every step and everywhere, the irrational momentum of anonymous, impersonal and inhuman power – the power of ideologies, systems, apparat, bureaucracy, artificial languages, and political slogans.[41]

Secondly, through the dialogue the peace movement was able to expand the space in which the East European groups operated and to assist communication between them. In part, the peace movement represented an inspiration to young people who wanted to be able to demonstrate as in the West. As one young pastor put it at the Dresden Peace Forum in 1982:

> In our television news we see lengthy reports of West European peace movements; and there are many young people who ask why it is so difficult to do such things here. People want to know why, in this country, where there is after all so much talk of peace, wearing the 'Swords into Ploughshares' badge, for instance, can lead to so many difficulties.[42]

For many young people, a direct connection was made between the Cold War and their own situation. 'We have got used to a divided Europe,' one of the founders of the Hungarian group Dialogue wrote in 1983;

> it has become too much part of our consciousness, it does not even occur to us that it can be changed. I am afraid that this already absurd situation could deteriorate further. It would be unbearable to have closed borders, the halt of mutual commerce, hatred, preparations of one side against the other, and a national paranoia behind every critical voice.
>
> The fight to avoid and prevent this gives me a tangible purpose. Our first documents which came out after long discussion, indicate that we think of the Cold War as our primary enemy and the struggle and its style are indicated by one of the meanings of our name: Dialogue.[43]

But the peace movement also provided support and visibility to the groups in Central Europe and, in effect, acted as a kind of umbrella or a form of protection especially in Hungary and Czechoslovakia. In the GDR and Poland, the Churches were able to offer some shelter to the new groups; this was not possible in the other countries. In the end, the issue of how to relate to officials became a matter of necessity. Since the official peace committees had the job of liaising with Western peace groups, peace activists were able to make use of this privileged access and to put pressure on them to tolerate the existence of the East European groups, as in the case of Hungary.

By the end of the decade, the peace movement was able to facilitate East–East networking as well. It was often difficult for East European dissidents to travel and communicate even within the Soviet Empire; their methods of reaching each other often passed through London, Berlin or Stockholm. Indeed, these East–West as well as East–East links and connections had become so widespread by the late 1980s that a crackdown was becoming more and more difficult. It was the many small holes that penetrated the Cold War structures, said Jan Kavan, the former Czech Foreign Minister and President of the United Nations General Assembly, that helped to undermine the whole edifice.[44]

Finally, the endless negotiation and pressure on officials about travel or holding meetings or the release of individual activists did eventually begin to influence 'insiders' who contributed to the non-violent nature of the 1989 revolutions. 'It is like water dripping on a stone,' one official told me privately. It helped to undermine the ideology of the regimes. Above all, it helped to influence the 'new thinking' of the Gorbachev regime.[45]

It was the disarmament ideas that were the first to be adopted in the Soviet Union. The idea of 'reasonable sufficiency' meant that the Soviet Union could accept numerically asymmetric arms control agreements, since overkill was unnecessary – this led to a whole series of new agreements, particularly the INF Treaty of 1987, which ushered in a new era of détente. When Gorbachev effectively renounced the Brezhnev Doctrine, when his spokesman used the Frank Sinatra song 'I did it My Way' to explain the policy towards Eastern Europe, this was the signal for the revolutions to begin. The explicit links between peace and human rights, disarmament and democracy, or the idea of a Common European Home, were first expressed among the new groups that made their appearance with 'glasnost' (openness) and later were included in official speeches. They reflected the peace movement literature, and it was these ideas that contributed to the unravelling of Soviet ideology.

What the peace movement added to the ideas of the Central European intellectuals was transnationalism in practice (the real possibility of networks of citizens, which could cross borders and bore holes into closed societies) as well as alternative concepts of security. Together, they developed proposals for a new international framework, modelled on the Helsinki Agreement, within which the distinction between peace and human rights would be eroded. The new ideas were thus a combination of transnationalism or globalization and, at the same time, a new understanding and extension of democracy focusing on concepts like empowerment, participation and deliberation, which have become so important in the 1990s. Thus they were talking about transnational anti-politics or a parallel cosmopolis[46] or even global civil society. Indeed the term European civil society began to be used at the end of the 1980s.[47]

Social scientists will never agree about the relative importance of the different factors that led to the end of the Cold War. The significance of the 1989 revolutions will be perceived differently depending on underlying theoretical perspectives. But one test of a good explanation is its predictive power. Those who studied Eastern Europe 'from above', who studied economic trends or the composition of politburos, failed to predict the 1989 revolutions. In the aftermath of the revolutions, there was much soul-searching in think tanks across the United States in particular. Those who were engaged in the dialogue knew that change was under way; they did not predict the form of the 1989 revolutions but they did expect something to happen. Perhaps the most prescient person was E. P. Thompson. In 1982, he wrote:

> what we can glimpse now...is a détente of peoples rather than states – a movement of peoples which sometimes dislodges states from their blocs and brings them into a new diplomacy of conciliation, which sometimes runs beneath state structures, and which sometimes defies the ideological and security structures of particular states...
>
> The Cold War road show, which each year enlarges, is now lurching towards its terminus. But in this moment changes have arisen in our continent, of scarcely more than one year's growth, which signify a challenge to the Cold War itself. These are not 'political' changes in the usual sense. They cut through the flesh of politics down to the human bone...
>
> What I have proposed is improbable. But, if it commenced, it might gather pace with astonishing speed. There would not be decades of détente as the glaciers slowly melt. There would be

rapid and unpredictable changes; nations would become unglued from their alliances; there would be sharp conflicts within nations; there would be successive risks. We could roll up the map of the Cold War and travel without maps for a while.[48]

Conceptual implications

These new ideas and the new version of civil society have to be understood in terms of the changing character of political authority in the 1980s and 1990s. They were a reaction not just to the totalitarian state but to the rigidities of the international framework within which states were embedded. In this sense, they expressed the frustrations of ordinary people, not just in the East, where the situation seemed inexorable and unending, but in the West as well.

The national state was always an imperfect institution and, it can be argued, had begun to crack already by 1914 under the twin pressures of increasing interconnectedness of economies and societies and the difficulties of sustaining clear boundaries, and, at the same time, growing demands for emancipation, for further extensions of rights. Tilly points out that, although states now extend all over the world, this may be a case of Parkinson's Law that the perfect layout is achieved when an institution is on the point of collapse – a prime example being the British construction of an imperial capital in New Delhi completed just before Independence. 'States may be following the old routine by which an institution falls into ruin just as it becomes complete.'[49]

After two unbelievably barbaric wars in the twentieth century, it can be argued that a new form of political authority was developed, involving a mutation of the classic nation-state. This form was the blocs. Indeed, it is worth noting that, in the debates about the future of the nation-state and the impact of globalization, almost no account is taken of the fact that, long before the latest phase of globalization, profound changes were taking place in the character of states as a consequence of the bloc system.[50]

Basically, the blocs represented a reconstitution of the Great Divide. The blocs involved an extension of civil society, in the case of the West, or domestic peace across groups of nations. Violence was, as it were, pushed further outwards. At least in Europe, an important limitation on state sovereignty was introduced as a consequence of the integration and bloc-wide specialization of armed forces; individual states could no longer wage war unilaterally.[51] I have used the term 'imaginary war' to describe the Cold War.[52] It was a war sustained in our imaginations through the reproduction of an ever more fearsome military confrontation, through spying games and hostile rhetoric. We lived as though we were at war and the war shaped our membership in collectivities just as earlier wars had shaped the 'imagined communities' of the nation. For the West, the threat of nuclear war was justified by the absence of human rights in the East and the risk that totalitarianism might spread and for the East, the absence of human rights was justified by the permanent threat of war.

In the West, the blocs could be said to have involved an extension of the social contract or bargain – indeed, one might argue that the territorially based social contract reached its logical endpoint during the Cold War. As war became more extreme and terrible, so the price of participation had to be greatly increased. Essentially, during this period, there were unprecedented gains in economic and social rights. But the risks were also dramatically extended. The price of these gains during this period was readiness to risk a nuclear war, to be part of a bloc-wide collectivity and to participate in a war of unimaginable proportions. This was not just an implicit contract; it was the consequence of explicit political bargaining in the late 1940s. It underlay what is sometimes called the post-war settlement.[53] This bargaining resulted in the political compromises between Democrats and Republicans in the United States (the Democrats retained big government in exchange for an anti-communist crusade) and between Europe and America (the Social Democrats could come to power in exchange for excluding communists from power, and for agreeing to Nato and a liberal international economic order).[54] It can be argued that this bargain did represent profound limitations on democracy particularly in southern Europe and Germany, or in the United States during the McCarthy era, and particularly as concerned security issues; moreover, the stifling Cold War ideology narrowed the space for open and honest dialogue. This explains the preoccupations of the new social movements and particularly the peace movement with issues of participation, empowerment and deliberation.

Whereas in the West, the war system or the military industrial complex, as it became known, was only one element of society albeit with profound implications, in the East, it can be argued, the war system encompassed society so that individual identity

was permanently eclipsed. Indeed, what is known as state socialism is better understood as a war system – a society that is
permanently organized for war on the model of the Second
World War. Such societies are characterized by centralization,
discipline and vertical hierarchy, high levels of military spending,
and an ideology of permanent struggle against an external enemy.
It was the culmination of the extremist tendencies of modern war.
In other words, if the war system depended on a social bargain in
the West, it depended on coercion in the East, much as in earlier
periods, but on a far grander, more all-encompassing scale.[55] The
way in which war or the idea of war became primarily an excuse
for domestic consolidation was marvellously anticipated by
George Orwell in the book *1984*, which was widely read by East
European dissidents. When the hero of *1984*, Winston Smith,
reads the book which describes the system under which he lives,
he discovers that:

> War, it will be seen, is now a purely internal affair. In the past, the
> ruling groups of all countries, although they might recognise their
> common interest and limit the destructiveness of war, did fight
> against one another, and the victor always plundered the van-
> quished. In our own day, they are not fighting against one another
> at all. The war is waged by each ruling group against its subjects, and
> the object of war is not to make or prevent conquests of territory
> but to keep the structure of society intact.[56]

What the dialogue of the 1980s achieved was to undermine this
logic. By the end of the 1980s there was an increasingly shared
consensus that détente from above and from below provided a
framework for opening up Eastern Europe, for creating autonomous spaces and laying the basis for democratization, that weak-
ening of the war system was a precondition for independent
political claims. And, by the same token, the widening of the
spaces, the beginnings of the process of democratization was
clearly the most effective strategy for dismantling the structures
of the Cold War.

The dialogue thus expressed two important developments,
which can be explained under the rubric of the accelerating process of globalization. First of all, the social contract of the Cold
War period was beginning to break down. On the one hand, after
Vietnam, after the questionings of the new social movements

about the legacy of the Second World War, and after the anti-nuclear movements of the 1980s, the readiness to risk life in war was no longer automatic. Indeed, the case for war itself was called into question. The growing sense of common humanity that emerged out of the experience of these wars is part of the meaning of 'global', as I shall explore in subsequent chapters. On the other hand, the growing neoliberal consensus, the challenges to the Keynsian state, and the spread of globalization, in the sense of global capitalism, eroded the guarantee of economic and social rights.

Secondly, this was a period of growing interconnectedness. Even if email and Internet had not yet entered general use, cheaper travel, telephone and faxes were contributing to the collapse of the distinction between Western and non-Western societies. The capacity of non-Western states to sustain populist projects within closed societies has been undermined and this is one of the main lessons of 1989. Increasing interconnectedness at a political as well as a cultural level provides some protection for disaffected individuals and allows them to demand extensions of political and civil rights, which in turn contributes to a speeding up of globalization. As Beck puts it: 'The categories framing world society – the distinction between highly developed and under-developed countries, between tradition and modernity – are collapsing. In the cosmopolitan paradigm of second modernity, the non-western societies share the same space and time horizon with the West.'[57]

The collapse of these distinctions between Western and non-Western societies, between coercive-intensive societies and societies characterized by bargains and contracts, is also illustrated by the fact that many of the same ideas seem to have developed simultaneously in Latin America, particularly Brazil. I have not been able to discover any direct connection between thinkers in Latin America and Central Europe at that time; on the contrary, Latin American dissidents were generally left-wing and suspicious of East European dissidents (and vice versa). In Latin America, the term developed as a response to the 'bureaucratic-authoritarian' regimes dominated by the military and the ideology of National Security. In particular, in Brazil after 1974, when the military announced an 'abertura', a limited democratic opening, the term civil society spread dramatically. It became, in Alfred Stepan's words, the 'political celebrity of the abertura'.[58] According to

Fernando Cardoso (former President of Brazil): 'In Brazilian political language, everything which was an organised fragment was being designated *civil society*. Not rigorously, but effectively, the whole opposition...was being described as if it were the movement of Civil Society.'[59]

The Brazilian intellectuals, unlike their Central European counterparts, were explicitly influenced by Gramsci. But in the militaristic context of Latin America, the term came to reflect an emerging reality, which was reminiscent of the way it was used in Central Europe. Small groups had created islands of engagement much as in Central Europe, often under the umbrella of the Church. The Brazilian Francisco Weffort, in words which parallel those of Jacek Kuroń above, argues that civil society was the necessary discovery of the epoch:

> The discovery that there was something more to politics than the state began with the simplest facts of life of the persecuted. In the most difficult moments, they had to make use of what they found around them. There were no parties to go to, no courts in which they could have confidence. At a difficult time, the primary resource was the family, friends and in some cases a fellow worker. What are we talking about if not civil society, though still at the molecular level of interpersonal relations? In a situation of enormous ideological complexity, the discovery of civil society was much less a question of theory than of necessity.[60]

The term spread rapidly not only to other parts of Latin America but to Asia and Africa as well, often in the context of similar types of regime. It was not that the East Europeans invented a new form of politics. On the contrary, what was happening in Central Europe was also happening all over the world. Rather, because perhaps of the peculiar conditions of post-totalitarian societies, where it was possible to think but not to act, they invented a language and a discourse that seemed to explain and to express what others were doing. Neera Chandhoke, for example, describes the development of new social movements in India from the 1960s onwards – the Naxalites, the anti-caste movement, the women's movement, and, after the lifting of the Emergency, the civil liberties and environmental movement as well. These movements pioneered a new form of politics which broke the hegemony of the Congress Party, and which took place

outside formal party politics. 'Oddly enough,' writes Chandhoke
'the language of civil society, which as a product of specific historical processes in England and France is arguably an alien import,
proved particularly apt for societies, which were struggling to
consolidate fledgling democracies.'[61]

Likewise, civil society was an important concept in the developments that took place in South Africa in the last years of apartheid.
As in Central Europe, the term had a strong transnational element.
In Latin America and South Africa, North American and European
human rights groups, often the progeny of the new social movements, played a critical role in providing support, public pressure
and publicity where necessary.[62] The various international instruments, fashioned beneath the structures of the Cold War – the
Human Rights Conventions and other treaties – could be used to
question the role of the Cold War as a legitimating ideology not
only in Europe but in the rest of the world as well.

To conclude: My argument is that there were indeed new ideas
in the revolutions of 1989 and they can be summed up in the
concept of global civil society. What was new about the concept,
in comparison with earlier concepts of civil society, was both the
demand for a radical extension of both political and personal
rights – the demand for autonomy, self-organization or control
over life – and the global content of the concept. These were
demands both about going beyond the state and transforming
the state. To achieve these demands, the new civil society actors
found it necessary and possible to make alliances across borders
and to address not just the state but international institutions
as well.

It is worth noting that in all the thousands of pages that have
been written about the 1989 revolutions the global aspect both of
ideas and practice is generally neglected. This is partly because of
Western triumphalism and the fact that the ideas were taken up
by Westerners, like Garton Ash or Dahrendorf, who interpreted
them as what the West already had, and who had not yet begun to
think about globalization. It may also be because the dissidents did
not expect to take power; all their writings suggest that they
envisaged anti-politics and the parallel *polis* as long-term strategies
for transformation. When they did become politicians, their ideas
narrowed, although both Havel and Mazowiecki, the Polish
Catholic former Prime Minister, as well as others, have tried to
play a humanistic role on the world stage.

The year 1989 did represent a profound rupture with the past that is difficult for us to comprehend. In the stirrings of thought that developed beneath the structures of the Cold War were the beginnings of some new concepts and practices that can help us to analyse our immensely complex contemporary world. Perhaps the most important reason why it was so difficult to identify the new ideas of 1989 was that we had not come to terms with the radical changes currently taking place. We only had old situations, earlier revolutions, the simplicities of the past, by which to describe what was happening.

All the same, some of these ideas have echoed through the 1990s, especially among the successors of the movements that participated in 'détente from below'. The 1989 revolutions legitimated the concept of civil society and consequently permitted the emergence of global politics – the engagement of social movements, NGOs and networks in the process of constructing global governance. And the coming together of peace and human rights gave rise to the new humanitarian discourse that is challenging the geopolitical discourse of the centralized war-making state. These implications of the new ideas are drawn out in the next two chapters.

4
Social Movements, NGOs and Networks

Terms like 'global politics' or global civil society signify the domestication of the international. We are accustomed to think of the international as the realm of diplomacy, high-level meetings and military strategy and the domestic, at least in democratic societies, as the realm of debate, discussion and public pressure – in short, the realm of politics; that is the meaning of the Great Divide. The 'global scene', says Bauman, was traditionally 'the theatre of *inter-state*' relations. Then after the Second World War, the development of '*supra-state* integration', the emergence of blocs, not just East and West but also the non-aligned bloc, meant that the ' "global scene" was increasingly seen as the theatre of coexistence and competition between *groups of states*, rather than between states themselves'.[1]

The salient characteristic of the world after 1989 is the advent of politics in the 'global scene'. By global politics, I mean the interaction between the institutions of global governance (international institutions and states) and global civil society – the groups, networks and movements which comprise the mechanisms through which individuals negotiate and renegotiate social contracts or political bargains at a global level. In other words, a system of relations between states or groups of states, characterized by a process of bargaining based on collective interest, in which the threat of armed conflict was an ever-present characteristic of the bargaining, has been supplanted by a much more complex world of politics, involving a range of institutions and individuals and in which there is a place, perhaps small, for individual reason and sentiment, and not just state or bloc interest.

This development is the outcome of changes both from above and below. On the one hand, 1989 marked the end of global conflict, the disintegration of blocs and the end of the prevalent use of ideology to suppress critical voices or even just good-tempered conversation at the international level. This made it possible for states and international institutions to deal with each other in new cooperative and discursive ways that were more receptive to individuals and citizens groups outside the corridors of power. On the other hand, the movements and groups who had struggled for peace and democracy or for human rights and environmental responsibility during the Cold War years were able to take advantage of this new openness as well as the ways in which the new language of global civil society legitimized their activities.

A theme of this chapter is that this process involved what I call the 'taming' of the social movements of the pre-1989 period. Their successors, I argue, are what are known as NGOs. The growing dominance of NGOs, together with the rise of new nationalist and religious movements and the decline of many older civic associations like trade unions, has tempered the initial enthusiasm for the language of civil society, at least among activists.

There is today a proliferation of language used to describe the non-state actors in global politics: global social movements;[2] international NGOs (INGOs); transnational advocacy networks;[3] civil society organizations; global public policy networks;[4] to name but a few. I use the term global civil society, as set out in chapter 2, to describe the global process through which individuals debate, influence and negotiate an ongoing social contract or set of contracts with the centres of political and economic authority. In other words, global civil society includes all those organizations, formal and informal, which individuals can join and through which their voices can be heard by decision-makers. In this chapter, I develop a typology of the main ways in which global civil society is organized, which is summarized in table 4.1. These are in effect ideal types; it is always possible to identify organizations which do not fit neatly into one category or which have overlapping characteristics.

In elaborating this typology, I do not draw a strict distinction between what is 'national' and what is 'global'; indeed the central thrust of my argument is that those distinctions no longer make

Table 4.1 A typology of global civil society actors

	'Old' social movements pre-1970	'New' social movements c.1970s and 1980s	NGOs, think-tanks, commissions c. late 1980s and 1990s	Transnational civic networks c. late 1980s and 1990s	'New' nationalist and fundamentalist movements 1990s	'New' anti-capitalist movement c. late 1990s and 2000s
Issues	Redistribution, employment and welfare; self-determination and anti-colonialism	Human rights; peace; women; environment; third world solidarity	Human rights; development and poverty reduction; humanitarianism; conflict resolution	Women; dams; land mines; international criminal court; global climate change	Identity politics	Solidarity with victims of globalization; abolition or reform of global institutions
Social composition	Workers and intellectuals	Students, new information class, caring professions	Professionals and experts	Professionals, experts and activists	Workers, small entrepreneurs, farmers, informal sector	Students, workers and peasants
Forms of organization	Vertical, hierarchical	Loose, horizontal coalitions	Ranges from bureaucratic and corporate to small-scale and informal	Networks of NGOs, social movements and grass roots groups	Vertical and horizontal, charismatic leadership	Networks of NGOs, social movements, and grass roots groups

Forms of action	Petition, demonstration, strike, lobbying	Use of media; direct action	Service provision; advocacy; expert knowledge; use of media	Parallel summits; use of media; use of local and expert knowledge; advocacy	Media, mass rallies, violence	Parallel summits; direct action, use of media; mobilization through internet
Funding	Membership	Individual supporters; events like concerts	Governments; international institutions; private foundations	Individual supporters; private foundations; INGOs	Diaspora; criminal activities	Individual supporters; churches; private foundations
Relation to power	Capturing state power	Changing state/society relations	Influencing civil society, the state and international institutions	Pressure on states and international institutions	Capturing state power	Confrontation with states, international institutions and transnational corporations

sense. Although it is possible, for example, to focus on International NGOs (INGOs), that is to say NGOs registered as international organizations, and I do provide some data about their growth, this does not, by a long way, cover all the NGOs that have some form of global connection. Indeed almost all social movements and NGOs, including parochially minded nationalist and religious groups, have some kind of transnational relations. Precisely because these groups inhabit a political space outside formal national politics (parties and elections), they address a range of institutions (local, global and national), they operate through links with a range of international institutions (NGOs, inter-governmental organizations, foreign states, Diaspora groups) and they often receive funding from abroad.

'Old' and 'new' social movements

The first two types of actor are what are called 'old' and 'new' social movements. Like civil society, there is a range of definitions of social movements but it is generally agreed that social movements are organizations, groups of people and individuals, who act together to bring about transformation in society. They are contrasted with, for example, more tightly organized NGOs or political parties. Tarrow says that social movements are an 'invention of the modern age and an accompaniment to the rise of the modern state'.[5] At the base of all social movements are what he calls 'contentious politics' – action, which is 'used by people who lack regular access to institutions, who act in the name of new or unaccepted claims and who behave in ways that fundamentally challenge others or authorities'.[6] There has always been contentious politics but social movements can be described as the modern form of contentious politics. Tilly talks about the contrast in repertoires between traditional and modern protests.[7] He uses the term 'repertoire' to resolve the tension between structure and agency, between protest as a deterministic response to structural conflict or malfunctions in society, and protest as a conscious individualistic act. Protests are an expression of human agency, of the will of the participants, but they are constrained by frameworks inherited from the past. Thus the repertoire of social movements can be distinguished from earlier forms of protest, according to Tilly, in three respects:

- They are 'cosmopolitan' rather than parochial, that is to say, they are concerned with issues and principles that apply to human beings in general and not just to their own interests in a particular locality. Tarrow cites the amazement of the Jamaican sugar lobby when the first great petition against slavery was circulated in 1788: 'these abolitionists had neither been injured by slavery nor would they personally benefit from its end; what right had they to petition for its abolition?'[8]
- They are 'autonomous' rather than bifurcated; that is to say individuals form organizations through which they can directly address the relevant authorities, in contrast to pre-modern or early modern forms of protest where individuals addressed a local patron or authority even where the issues were of more than local significance.
- They are 'modular' rather than particular, that is to say, they develop routines of protest, like the petition, the strike or the demonstration, that are easily transferable to different situations, in contrast to traditional protests like grain seizures or rick burnings that varied from issue to issue and locality to locality.

One might add a further difference. Traditional protests were often violent. The rise of social movements involves a 'civilizing' of protest.[9] Even though social movements may break the law, through various forms of direct action or civil disobedience, non-violence has become a dominant commitment of contemporary social movements, at least until the recent anti-capitalist actions.

Social movements rise and fall. Their success depends both on their capacity to mobilize and on the responsiveness of authorities. To the extent that authorities permit protest and take seriously the demands of the protestors, then social movements are 'tamed', integrated into the political process and institutionalized. 'Taming' is not just about access; it is about adaptation on both sides. The authorities accept part of the agenda of protest; the movements modify their goals and become respectable. To the extent that authorities repress protest and reject demands, social movements are marginalized and may turn to violence. Tarrow talks about cycles of contention; although the endings may differ, social movements do always come to an end:

Each time they appear, the world seems to be turning upside down. But just as regularly, the erosion of mobilisation, the polarisation

between sectors of the movements, the splits between institutionalisation and violence, and elites' selective use of incentives and
repression combine to bring the cycle to an end. At its height, the
movement is electric and seems irresistible, but it is eroded and
integrated through the political process.[10]

Or, as Rob Walker argues, the point of social movements is that
they move:

> They come and go, rise and decline, provoke a fuss and wither on
> the vine. They take the familiar path from charisma to regularised
> routine, from inventiveness and passion to bureaucracy, hierarchy
> and instrumental reason. Or alternatively, they fracture, mutate,
> dissipate, gather no moss. To be in motion is to be at odds with
> many of the criteria on which serious politics has come to be
> judged.[11]

The literature on social movements tends to distinguish between
'old' and 'new' social movements, as in table 4.1. 'Old' movements tend to be labour movements or movements for self-
determination, as in the case of nineteenth-century national
movements or anti-colonial movements. They were mass membership movements that addressed the state and were organized
hierarchically, with executive committees and chairmen and
secretary-generals. They used the modern repertoire of protest –
petitions, demonstrations and strikes. 'New' social movements are
generally considered to be the offspring of the 1968 student
revolutions. They are concerned with new issues – human rights,
gender, the environment or peace. They express the political
frustrations of a new educated middle class or brain workers –
ICT (Information and Communications Technology) specialists or
the caring professions (doctors, lecturers, social workers) generated by post-industrialism and the welfare state.[12] They pioneer
new forms of horizontal organization and new forms of protest,
making use of the media, especially television. Whereas the 'old'
movements aimed at persuading states to act and in the process
helped to strengthen them, the 'new' movements are much more
concerned about individual autonomy, about resisting the state's
intrusion into everyday life.[13] Claus Offe has argued that the
'new' movements represent a demand for radical democracy.
'Among the principal innovations of the new movements, in con-

trast with the workers' movement, are a critical ideology in relation to modernism and progress; decentralised and participatory
organisational structures; defence of interpersonal solidarity
against the great bureaucracies; and the reclamation of autonomous spaces rather than material advantages.'[14]

The new social movements, from the beginning, have been a
global phenomenon. The 1970s and 1980s witnessed the emergence of human rights groups, environmental groups, or women's
groups in Latin America, Asia and Africa as well.[15] Rajni Kothari,
writing in the late 1980s, described this new phenomenon of the
'non-party political process' – the 'churning of civic consciousness'
– in India. The response of spontaneous citizens' initiatives to the
Bhopal disaster, to the anti-Sikh pogroms after the assassination of
Mrs Gandhi, or the support for struggles like those of people in
the Narmada valley or the Chipko movement, are all examples of
what he calls 'islands of hope'. 'The new social groups and movements,' writes Kothari, in words that would be familiar to East
and West Europeans as well as to Latin Americans and Africans,
'whether of peasants or environmentalists, or the new breed of
human rights and civil liberties movements, or the ethnic movements among the minorities, or the whole new upsurge of women
– this is a whole new space. It is a different space, which is
essentially a non-party space. Its role is to deepen the democratic
process in response to the state that has not only ditched the poor
and oppressed but has itself turned oppressive and violent. It is to
highlight dimensions that were not hitherto considered political
and make them part of the political process.'[16]

It is sometimes also argued that the 'old' movements are
'national' in contrast to the cosmopolitan character of the 'new'
social movements.[17] But Tilly is right to characterize the modern
repertoire as 'cosmopolitan'. The 'old' movements were not
originally national. The various movements that pressed for the
achievement of individual rights were always universalistic in
their aspirations, as I discussed in chapter 2. Likewise, the labour
movement was always an international movement. The first international of labour was held in 1864; workers travelled to different
countries to express solidarity with their fellow workers from the
late nineteenth century onwards; the International Federation of
Trade Unions was founded in 1901. The identification of 'old'
movements as national is the consequence of the cycle of contention. 'Old' movements did primarily address the state, although

not exclusively, but it was through the state that 'old' movements were 'tamed'. This was true both of workers' movements, which became left political parties and trade unions, and anti-colonial struggles, which were transformed into new ruling parties, as was the case for the Congress Party in India or is the case for the African National Congress in South Africa today. These movements were transformed into political parties and, in the case of trade unions, into negotiating partners for states and employers at a national level. The mass character of the 'old' movements, their vertical and hierarchical forms of organization, are all perhaps explainable in terms of the organizational norms of industrial, bureaucratic and military society.

NGOs

It can be argued that the third type of global civil society actor represents the 'taming' of the 'new' social movements. In contrast to 'old' social movements, the 'new' social movements were 'tamed' not within a national framework but within the framework of global governance. Compared with social movements, NGOs are institutional and generally professional; they include voluntary associations, charities, foundations, or professional societies and they are usually formally registered. Organizations can be defined as 'purposeful, role-bound social units'.[18] NGOs are organizations which are voluntary, in contrast to compulsory organizations like the state or some traditional, religious organizations, and do not make profits, like corporations. It is sometimes said that they are 'value-driven' organizations.[19] In fact, values like public service, for example, or wealth creation, are also important for states and for corporations. Rather, it could be said that, in any organization, both internal relationships and relations with external actors are regulated through a combination of coercion, monetary incentives and altruism (or values). In the case of NGOs, the latter is relatively more important.

NGOs are not new, although the term is relatively recent; non-governmental organizations are mentioned in Article 71 of the UN Charter, where the Economic and Social Committee is empowered 'to make suitable arrangements for consultation with non-governmental organisations which are concerned with matters in its competence'.[20] Already, international NGOs

(INGOs) were established in the nineteenth century. The most famous examples are probably the Anti-Slavery Society (1839) and the International Red Cross (1864). By 1874, there were thirty-two registered INGOs and this had increased to 1,083 by 1914 although not all survived.[21] INGOs were instrumental in setting up international institutions during this period, many of which began as non-governmental institutions.[22] They also influenced treaty-making, particularly in the case of anti-slavery, and many of the techniques that INGOs use today were pioneered during this period, particularly parallel fora at inter-governmental conferences. The Hague Peace Conferences of 1899 and 1907 were particularly significant in this respect where NGOs organized parallel sessions and even published an unofficial newspaper.[23]

In the inter-war period, INGOs were very active in the League of Nations up to 1935 and in the International Labour Organization, which even today includes delegates from trade unions, employer organizations and women's groups in its formal structures, alongside governmental organizations. According to Charnowitz, the two most influential groups were the Women's International League for Peace and Freedom (WILPF), founded in the First World War, which moved its headquarters to Geneva, and the International Chamber of Commerce.[24]

The number of INGOs increased during the post-war period not only under the stimulation of new social movements but also as former missionaries and colonial administrators sought new occupations. In the 1950s and 1960s, however, their influence was constrained by the Cold War and the statist character of many of the post-war international institutions. It was not until the 1970s that the opening up of access for 'new' social movements to local and international institutions led to the proliferation of both NGOs in general and INGOs in particular. Initially, this opening up applied mainly to 'soft' issues that did not seem to engage directly with the ideological conflict, mainly the environment and women. The Stockholm Conference on Environment and Development in 1972 marked the beginning of the parallel summit as a way of organizing global civil society organizations on particular issues. Likewise, a series of world conferences on women helped to galvanize women's groups – Mexico City 1975, Copenhagen 1980, Nairobi 1985 and Beijing 1995.[25] By the 1980s, development and humanitarian INGOs also began to be seen as partners for governments and international institutions for a variety of reasons: their local knowledge, the need to bypass ineffective or authoritarian governments, and the need to find ways to implement structural adjustment packages.

The end of the Cold War accelerated these tendencies. It was no longer possible to ally with authoritarian governments in the context of a wave of support for democratization and human rights. As the ideological conflict dissolved, governments and international institutions became more responsive to peace and human rights groups. A number of writers stress the importance of the 'New Policy Agenda', which came to prominence after the end of the Cold War. The 'New Policy Agenda' combined neoliberal economic strategy with an emphasis on parliamentary democracy. Already in the 1980s, the World Bank had established an NGO – World Bank Committee. Markets plus elections became the ideological formula of the 1990s. NGOs came to be seen as an important mechanism for implementing this agenda. They can provide a social safety net without extending the role of the government. They can provide training in democracy and citizenship. They can check abuses of the state and poor governmental practices. And they can push corporations towards an agenda of social responsibility. Concepts like 'social capital' (Putnam) or 'trust' (Fukuyama) contributed to the new-found enthusiasm for NGOs both by development institutions like the World Bank and in the peace and human rights field. Moreover, in the second half of the 1990s, 'third way' politicians came to power in Western Europe who accepted the neoliberal orthodoxy, but nevertheless had learned their politics through the experience of new social movements and were ready to pursue new issues and to open up the corridors of power to 'tamed' social movements. Finally, as the immediate post-Cold War neoliberal triumphalism was blunted towards the end of the 1990s, even the hard-core international institutions like the IMF began a dialogue with INGOs.[26]

These openings have encouraged institutionalization and professionalization, the transformation of social movements into NGOs or INGOs. Lester Salamon has described the dramatic growth of NGOs in the 1980s and 1990s as the 'global associational revolution'. The Johns Hopkins Survey of the non-profit sector in twenty-two countries shows that this sector contributed significantly to employment growth in the 1980s and 1990s. The sector accounted for some 5.1 per cent of total employment in the countries surveyed and some 10.4 million volunteers, bringing the total to 7.1 per cent of total employment.[27] The same rapid increase can be found among NGOs registered as international organizations. During the 1990s, registered INGOs increased by one third, from 10,292 to 13,206, and their memberships increased from 155,000 to 263,000 over the same period.[28] A major factor in the growth of NGOs has been the increase in official funding. OECD (Organization for Economic Cooperation and Development) figures show that by the end of the 1990s, some 5 per cent of all official aid was channelled through NGOs, with differing shares for different countries. Some 85 per cent of Swedish aid is channelled through NGOs and some 10 per cent of UK aid.[29]

These overall figures conceal the very wide differences between NGOs and the changing composition of NGOs. The term NGO includes those organizations that are typically considered NGOs, international NGOs (INGOs) like Oxfam, Amnesty International or Greenpeace, that are organized around a particular cause – poverty, human rights, or protection of the environment. But it also includes professional societies and self-help groups, like trade unions, sporting groups, or refugee organizations. And it includes those organizations that are sometimes called community building groups (CBOs) or grass roots organizations (GROs) that may be informal and local. Some organizations are very big and similar to large companies; in the development and humanitarian field, for example, there are some eight market leaders, each with a budget of roughly $500 million a year; they include famous names like Oxfam, Médecins sans Frontières, Save the Children or CARE (Cooperative for American Relief Everywhere).[30] Others may be small, self-organized and spontaneous.

As a consequence of their 'tamed' character, NGOs are able to act as interlocutors on issues with which new social movements are concerned. In addition, many have built up expert knowledge on particular policy areas, which enables them to challenge the official experts. This is why I have included think tanks and international commissions in this category. Like many of the NGOs, think tanks are a source of alternative expert knowledge. International commissions are another 'taming' device in which independent groups of prominent individuals and experts are brought together to produce reports on issues of global significance. The

Brandt, Palme and Brundtland Commissions pioneered this approach on development, security and the environment respectively. In the 1990s, this type of commission has proliferated – for example, the World Commission on Dams (WCD), the Kosovo Commission, or the two Carnegie Commissions on the Balkans and on Deadly Conflicts.

A subset of this category, which is rarely mentioned in the literature on global civil society but which is nevertheless extremely powerful, are the think tanks, like the American Enterprise Institute or the Centre for Civil Society in India, and lobbying organizations allied to transnational business. These groups have a much longer history of access to official agencies and have been much more successful than other INGOs in getting their proposals on to the global policy agenda.[31]

It is possible to identify four main differences among NGOs, which have affected their overall composition. The four are detailed below.

Northern versus southern NGOs   Since many northern NGOs are set up to assist people in the South, a distinction is often drawn between northern and southern NGOs and often equated with the distinction between NGOs and GROs or CBOs. In fact some southern NGOs are extremely large like the Bangladesh Rural Advancement Committee (BRAC) and there are many local community groups in advanced industrial countries which could be categorized as CBOs and GROs. The point of the distinction, however, is primarily about the contrast between NGOs who are outsiders and, at the same time, are closer to the policy-making community as well as to the sources of funds, and those NGOs more rooted in the local environment.

Advocacy versus service provision   NGOs undertake a wide variety of tasks, not all of which are captured by the headings 'advocacy' and 'service provision'. Service provision includes relief in emergencies, primary health care, non-formal education, housing and legal services, and provision of micro-credit, as well as training to other service providers. Advocacy includes lobbying as well as public mobilization and campaigning around particular issues like debt relief or the Tobin tax or protection of forests. And then there are a range of activities which can be included under both headings like monitoring compliance with international treaties, particularly in the human rights field, conflict resolution and reconciliation, public education and the provision of alternative expert knowledge. Service provision and the middle range of activities have become more important in the 1990s as donors have contracted or encouraged NGOs to fill the gaps created by the withdrawal of the state from many public services.

Solidarity versus mutual benefit Some NGOs are established to express solidarity with others. Thus Oxfam was established to help poor people in the third world; Amnesty International was established to help political prisoners. Typically solidaristic NGOs are organizations dependent on outside funding, whose members are committed individuals, often from the middle classes. They do not represent the poor and the deprived although their staff and members care about the poor and the deprived. Mutual benefit NGOs are formed for the mutual benefit of the members like, for example SEWA, the Self-employed Women's Association in India. Professional societies are typical mutual benefit organizations. The composition of mutual benefit NGOs tends to reflect the structure of society and it changes as society changes. The period of the 1990s has been a period of rapid structural change both because of globalization and IMF (International Monetary Fund) policies, and because of rapid technological change, especially the introduction of ICT. Many of the traditional mutual benefit organizations have been eroded and their political links broken; this is especially true of trade unions and farmers' organizations. On the other hand, new organizations have been developing to defend the rights of the victims of rapid structural change, although these, of course, are as yet weak. Such groups include movements of people in areas threatened by dam construction, like the Narmada valley, new organizations of informal workers, organizations of refugees and displaced persons like the Srebrenica women.

Organizational forms There are wide differences among NGOs concerning their forms of organization – formal versus informal, hierarchy versus participation, networks versus federations, centralized versus decentralization, not to mention differences of organizational culture. Some NGOs are membership organizations; others are governed by boards or trustees. Moreover, the meaning of membership varies. In Amnesty International, for example, the members are the 'owners' of the organization and determine its decision-making. By contrast, the members of Greenpeace are more like supporters passively donating money and numbers. Some NGOs organize themselves on bureaucratic principles; others are more corporate in management style. Transnationalization and the growing use of ICT does tend to favour decentralized, network-type organizations. There is some evidence that NGOs are currently going through a rapid period of experimentation with organizational forms; the statistics seem to suggest a growing share of NGOs whose organizational forms cannot be classified.[32]

The growing use of the term 'NGO' reflects what has been described as the 'NGOization' of public space. Effectively, what this means is that those NGOs who are northern and therefore close to the centres of power and funding, whose emphasis is service provision, who are solidaristic rather than mutual benefit, and whose organization tends to be more formal and hierarchical, have come to dominate the NGO scene. This is, in part, a consequence of the growing support of northern governments towards NGOs: they tend to favour service provision and may be nervous about advocacy; they are biased towards NGOs from their own countries and also prefer to deal with formally organized professional NGOs. And it is partly a consequence of rapid structural change, which has eroded traditional mutual benefit organizations as well as the kind of local community ties which help to foster GROs and CBOs.

The growth of this type of NGOs has given rise to widespread criticism of NGOs especially in Africa, Latin America and South Asia. First of all, it is argued that growing dependence on particular donors may distort the priorities or mission of NGOs. Dependence on government funding has, in some cases, transformed NGOs into parastatal organizations, or government subcontractors. In some cases, they have become substitutes for the state; since NGOs can bypass formal mechanisms of democratic accountability, they may reduce rather than enhance the power of citizens. Bangladesh, where NGOs have become such important actors, has been described as the 'Franchise State'.[33] It can also lead to a damping down of the advocacy role of NGOs since NGOs are fearful of losing their sources of income; in Afghanistan, for example, no American NGO even questioned the official air drop of humanitarian supplies, although European NGOs did so. Advocacy may also be weakened because powerful government-funded NGOs may displace local GROs and CBOs, as has been observed in Latin America and India.[34] In extreme cases, it is argued that NGOs are merely the 'handmaidens of capitalist change', with little serious concern for effective poverty alleviation strategies. They are seen as the 'modernisers and destroyers of local economies', introducing Western values and bringing about 'economicide'.[35]

This problem is exacerbated by the decline of many traditional mutual benefit organizations, like professional associations as a consequence of structural change. In the case of Africa, Gymah-Boadi has argued that 'Civil associations of all kinds have seen their material bases of support eroded, first by the protracted economic crisis that gripped Africa starting in the 1980s and then by stringent neo-liberal adjustment measures intended to resolve it. Many associations have lost so much self-confidence and organisational capacity that they seem but shadows of what they were a decade ago. Neopatrimonial leaders, meanwhile, find them easy targets for co-option. Faced with the prospect of penury, many leaders of middle-class and professional groups find it hard to resist making personally advantageous deals with incumbent autocratic regimes, even if such deals undermine pro-democracy movements and shore up authoritarian rule.'[36] Patrick Chabal suggests that, in the context of patrimonial states, NGOs created by Western donors 'are often nothing other than the new "structures" with which Africans can seek to establish an instrumentally profitable position within the existing system of patrimonialism'.[37] And in much of the post-communist world, NGOs provide a fund-raising channel for impoverished professionals or aspiring politicians.

A parallel argument is made about newly emerging relations between NGOs and companies. As part of the new commitment to social responsibility, companies undertake social and environmental programmes through subcontracting NGOs. It is sometimes argued that NGOs who implement this type of programme are contributing to what is essentially a public relations exercise where 'good works' conceal the longer-term strategic damage inflicted by the companies. According to this line of argument, oil companies in Nigeria and Angola, for example, undertake this type of programme, while, at the same time, oil revenues are fuelling conflict, and oil exploitation, however well managed, is contributing to environmental degradation.

Another criticism levelled at NGOs is that the growth of the predominant type of northern NGO has led to an intense competition – an emerging 'marketplace of ideas, funders, backers and supporters'.[38] To sustain themselves financially, NGOs need to identify a market niche, and to distinguish the NGO's brand name from others. This contradicts the cooperative practices, which ought to and often do take place as a consequence of the normative character of the mission, the value-driven nature of NGOs. As Fowler puts it:

> Increasing market profile and income share is now a common concern of Northern NGDO's [non-governmental development organizations] fundraising; overstating impact is widespread; distortions in fund-raising images are a frequent complaint of NGDOs from the South and East; and the lack of transparency is a source of disquiet in development circles and the media.[39]

In the NGO marketplace, media coverage is all important. A particular problem arises from the dependence of NGOs on media coverage. There is a tendency to exaggerate crises in order to mobilize public support, as in the case of Greenpeace and Brent Spa or the crisis in Eastern Zaire in 1995 or in some cases of GM crops.[40] And this is often encouraged by the media in search of newsworthy stories. As George Alagiah of the BBC put it: 'Relief agencies depend upon us for publicity and we need them to tell us where the stories are. There's an unspoken understanding between us, a sort of code. We try not to ask the question too bluntly: "Where are the starving babies?". And they never answer explicitly. But we get the pictures all the same.'[41]

In short, NGOs can be considered to be the 'tamed' successors of the 'new' social movements of the 1970s and 1980s. 'Taming' can range from co-option to autonomy. Perhaps NGOs could be described as a new sort of intermediary organization, an expression of the blurred boundaries between state and non-state, public and private. One way to describe them is in terms of the emergence of a flexible state, a mechanism through which states can adjust more rapidly to changes in society than is possible within the traditional bureaucratic model of the state. Another way to describe them is in terms of the extension of market principles throughout society, with the emphasis on competition and the idea of public–private partnerships. Nevertheless, they still remain 'value-driven' organizations and, even if they do not live up to expectations, they continue to be organized around humanistic missions. Even though they work with states and companies, most NGOs do retain a strong sense of their original mission and past practice, and many continue to provide an infrastructure which can be used by a range of social movements and grass roots organizations.

Transnational civic networks

The fourth category in my typology is global civic networks. These are networks that connect INGOs, social movements and grass roots organizations, as well as individuals on specific issues and campaigns. 'Détente from below' described in the last chapter can be understood as the construction of a transnational civic network. Likewise, campaigns about human rights, violence against women or the environment, during the 1980s, pioneered the contemporary form of network, although the precedents had been set much earlier. Keck and Sikkink use the term 'transnational advocacy network' and their networks include states and international organizations as well.[42]

Networks, says Castells, are the 'new social morphology' of the contemporary era[43]. They are flexible, fluid and they provide an opportunity for the voices of grass roots groups to be heard. They are forms of communication and information exchange; mutual discussion and debate transform the way issues are understood and the language within which they are expressed. They represent a kind of two-way street between southern groups and individuals, or rather the groups and individuals who directly represent victims, whether it be the victims of human rights violations, poverty or environmental degradation, with the so-called northern solidaristic 'outsiders'. The former provide testimony, stories and information about their situation and they confer legitimacy on those who campaign on their behalf. The latter provide access to global institutions, funders or global media as well as 'interpretations' more suited to the global context. Another way of describing this collaboration is in terms of the link between 'tamed' organizations and more activist groups; the latter tend to be more innovative and agenda-setting, while the former can professionalize and insti-tutionalize campaigns.

Keck and Sikkink have coined the term, the 'boomerang effect', whereby local groups, blocked at a national level, can use the network to influence other states and international organizations to unblock the national situation.[44] Thus the AIDs/HIV network has been successful in pressing for cheaper drugs as a result of a global campaign against (and sometimes in cooperation with) states, international organizations and pharmaceutical companies. A particularly important form of the 'boomerang effect' lies in the existence of international rules to which states have subscribed, like the 1975 Helsinki Agreement or the US Congressional legislation on human rights violations in Latin America in the 1970s, which can be used by local groups as an instrument in their campaigns. Also important are inspirational events like the Nairobi and Beijing women's conferences. In Sierra Leone, for example, women's groups had always been active in the Churches, local communities or Descendants groups. But it was not until 1994 that they came together to establish the Women's Forum, in order to prepare for the United Nations' Women's Conference in Beijing, with international support. This was the moment they became aware of their potential power and some of the women argued for a more political stance and, in particular, the need for women to play a role in securing peace. As a result the Sierra Leonean women's peace movement was formed, which was to have a decisive influence on the democratization process in 1995.[45]

It might be more appropriate to talk about a 'double boomer-ang' effect since the consequences of these local actions are often to strengthen international instruments as well, which can then be used to enhance local campaigns. Particularly important in the 1990s, for example, has been the influence of networks on inter-national treaty making: Land Mines, the International Criminal Court or Global Climate Change. What has been new since the end of the Second World War has been the development of humanitarian or cosmopolitan law that applies to individuals and not just states and is about setting norms in global affairs. Pressure from civic networks organized specifically for the purpose, as I argue in the next chapter, has been critical to this development.[46]

Transnational civic networks are not necessarily harmonious, democratic or effective. They represent a space for interchange which is often acrimonious and sometimes disillusioning. Southern NGOs often complain of being steamrollered. Indigenous peoples' groups are uncomfortable with the individualistic assumptions of northern groups, while the latter are often concerned about the patriarchal communitarian tendencies of southern groups. Focus and effectiveness in campaigning often overrides democratic and participatory ways of working. Nevertheless, especially in the last decade, such networks have had a considerable impact in transforming the normative content of global politics.

'New' nationalist and fundamentalist movements

Just as the new social movements were being tamed and as transnational civic networks were learning to act in the global arena, however, a new family of social movement developed – the 'new' nationalist or fundamentalist movements. These include exclusive nationalist movements in the Balkans and much of the postcommunist world, religious communalism (both Islamic and Hindu) in the Middle East and Asia, millennial or 'new age' movements in Africa and the United States, or the growing anti-immigrant movements in Western Europe.

In some respects, these movements are similar to 'old' social movements, in that they are often mass movements, which include workers and peasants; they are organized, at least in part, in traditional hierarchical ways, often with a charismatic leader; and their aim is most often to capture state power. But they differ from 'old' nationalist, labour and anti-colonial movements in several respects. First, they tend to be about the claim to power on the basis of labels rather than ideas. In the case of ethnic nationalist movements, this means that they make claims to political power on the basis of an ethnic label which excludes and is indeed hostile towards others with a different label. Or in the case of religious fundamentalist movements, they make claims to political power on the basis of religious practice, which also excludes others with different or non-religious practices.

Earlier nationalisms were typically about defining a nation as the basis for citizenship and, in the case of civic nationalisms, citizenship was a matter of residency, not cultural background or language, even though these had to be learned. In particular, self-determination or anti-colonial movements were about democracy, participation and rights, not about ethnicity or religion; they tended to be about a vision of nation-building. There have, of course, been ethnic nationalist movements in the past, like Zionism or Greek nationalism, and these movements have shared many of the characteristics of contemporary movements although they also had their progressive forward-looking projects about democracy and nation-building. Likewise, earlier religious struggles were about new visions of society – the role of the individual or the power of institutionalized religion – although they, also, had their fundamentalist wings. In Northern Ireland or the former Yugoslavia, religious struggles have little to do with beliefs; they are about access to political power.

There are many similarities between extreme ethnic chauvinism and religious fundamentalism. Both tend to be backward-looking; they appeal to those disaffected with materialism and corruption. They conjure up an idea of a pure traditional way of life – nostalgia for a past where supposedly this existed. Both emphasize violent forms of struggle and celebrate histories of bloody battles lost or won. Both are forms of identity politics, by which I mean the claim to power on the basis of identity, i.e. labels. Fundamentalist or extremist identity politics involve exclusive claims to power in the name of identity, i.e. the denial of the claims of other identities.

Some religious groups may also have a missionary character. By missionary character, I mean the effort to convert others and the insistence on the application of religious rules. Different Islamic groups, for example, distinguish themselves in terms of the way they interpret scriptures and Islamic Law. Thus al-Qaeda bases its ideology on Wahabi – an austere branch of Sunni, practised in Saudi Arabia and also Chechnya, in which non-Wahabi are equated with non-believers. They distinguish themselves from other Sunni groups, as well as, of course, from Shias. Nevertheless, the primary goal, as with other Islamic groups, is power, not the spread of religion. Al-Qaeda is linked to disaffected members of the Saudi royal family. The stated goal is a Muslim caliphate (state) in the whole of the Middle East but, undoubtedly, there is an underlying interest in power in Saudi Arabia. As Fred Halliday puts it: 'Religious fundamentalism in all societies has . . . one goal; this goes for the *haredim* in Israel, the ranting bible-thumpers of America, Islamic fundamentalists in the Middle East and Hindu chauvinists in India. The goal is not to convert other people to their beliefs, but to seize power, political, social and gendered, within their own societies.'[47]

The 'new' nationalist and religious movements tend to represent themselves as a reaction against modernity, as opposed to 'old' nationalist movements that saw themselves as agents of progress, building the modern state. Indeed, the new nationalism and religious fundamentalism could be viewed as ways of mobilizing *against* democracy and openness.

A second difference has to do with social composition. The new nationalist and fundamentalist movements have a capacity to mobilize workers and peasants, as was the case for 'old' social movements. But these groups are shrinking as a proportion of society following the dramatic structural changes that have taken place as a consequence of globalization. Instead, an important constituency for these movements are those people who have been forced to migrate to urban conglomerations all over the world and who make a living in low-paid service jobs or on the margins of the formal economy in the growing 'grey' activities that are associated with globalization. These are uprooted people living with the frustrations both of insecurity and, especially important for the new generation of restless young men who join these movements, forced inactivity and loss of self-worth as a consequence of unemployment.

A third difference has to do with forms of organization. Many nationalist and religious political movements organize themselves on the model of former left political parties. This is the case for the post-communist nationalists in Eastern Europe and the Balkans and for Islamic parties or the BJP (Bharatiya Janata Party) in India. However, these movements also characteristically combine this form with the construction of networks. Ethnicity, like religion, is now transnational. Both religious and nationalist movements have constituencies that cross borders. For nationalist movements, both Diaspora groups and kin-based organizations are important elements in the support infrastructure, providing funds and other forms of assistance and acting as global lobbying groups. Likewise, religious institutions in different countries – mosques, synagogues, churches or temples – provide similar support to religious movements. Just as civic networks make use of the 'boomerang effect' so Croatians in Germany or Irish Americans, London-based mosques or North American 'new age' groups have a major role in enhancing the effectiveness of these movements through lobbying, raising public awareness or through financial and technical assistance. Nor are the networks merely transnational; they are also functional as well. Whereas 'old' movements were largely funded through membership and engaged in traditional forms of political action, the 'new' movements make a range of connections with criminal groups, mercenaries, security services, enterprises and banks, both as a form of funding and because of the way in which they engage in violent and coercive activities.

A fourth difference has to do with the way the 'new' nationalist and fundamentalist movements have adapted some of the repertoire of the 'new' social movements. In particular, they engage in symbolic politics of a destructive and powerful kind, like the destruction of the Ayodha Mosque in India in 1992, or the Taliban's destruction of the stone sculptures of Buddha. Like the 'new' social movements, they place considerable emphasis on media impact, making use of television, radio, websites and videos. Videocassettes of Bin Laden's speeches circulate throughout the Middle East. The attacks on the World Trade Center and the Pentagon on September 11 represent a devastating example of symbolic, media-conscious, public and deliberately nihilistic action.[48]

The weakness of both 'new' social movements and NGOs is that although they have widespread moral authority, they are largely composed of an educated minority and they lack the capacity for popular mobilization. They are often part of the class of informational 'haves' – they have credit cards and access to the Internet and satellite television, they can afford to travel and meet each other. The 'new' nationalist movements appear to fill the gap left by the 'taming' of 'old' social movements and their virtual demise after the end of the Cold War. They can appeal to the 'ontological insecurity' of the 'have-nots' – those who are excluded from the new global class built upon global financial transactions, global communication and air travel, but nevertheless are deeply affected by the changes wrought by these developments. It is the nationalist and fundamentalist movements, not the democratic movements, that seem better able to capture popular sentiment, at least in some parts of the world.

Not all nationalist and religious groups, of course, are exclusivist and extremist. I have focused on this type of movement because of its importance at the beginning of the twenty-first century.

Apart from movements concerned with cultural or religious freedoms, or streams of religious thinking like liberal Islam or liberation theology, which have contributed to the development of humanistic norms, an important category of organization is the neo-traditional groups that provide welfare, religious instruction or even some form of security in many part of the world. They are often the main support networks and mobilizing mechanisms in, for example, newly urbanized poor neighbourhoods. These groups are often compulsory and communalist but they do not necessarily subscribe to nationalist and fundamentalist ideologies. They are often characterized by tolerance towards other parts of society and are even engaged in struggles for democratization, social advancement or environmental protection. It is these groups that have occasioned debate among the theorists of civil society, reflecting a real tension and ambivalence in their relationship to other civil society agents. Pearce and Howell describe these tensions between radical cultural and radical popular groups in relation to the Mayan people of Guatemala, who played such a key role in the democratization struggle under the banner of 'civil society'. 'On the one hand, civil society holds out a promise of freedom as it does for the popular sectors, on the other hand, it is not clear how associations now visibly trying to influence the state in the public political sphere relate to communal structures of indigenous villages.'[49]

The new anti-capitalist movement

The last category of global civil society actor is the 'new' anti-capitalist movement that burst into the streets of Seattle and Prague at the end of the decade. It is usually described as the anti-globalization movement but this is a misnomer as groups like 'globalize the resistance' or slogans like the 'world-wide movement against globalization' make clear. The term anti-capitalism is a more apt description since most of those engaged in the movement oppose the unregulated spread of capitalism and the growing power of the market over every aspect of life, and since it represents, in some respects, a revival of the great anti-capitalist movements of the late nineteenth and early twentieth centuries.[50] At the World Social Forum in Porto Alegre in 2002, the activists defined themselves as a 'global movement for social justice and solidarity'.[51]

The new anti-capitalist movement is similar in form to the global civic networks. But instead of being organized around a specific issue, it is a social movement in terms of its transformative goals. It is inspired by movements in poor countries like the Zapatistas, the landless peasant movement in Brazil, or the East Asian Third World Network. It brings together elements of the 'new' social movements and their 'tamed' successors – INGOs, networks and movements concerned with women's issues, the environment, or indigenous people's rights. But it also embraces the new mutual benefit organizations that are beginning to emerge in response to structural change – informal workers, refugees and displaced persons and so on, as well as what might be called the 'new' labour movement. The 'new' labour movement includes: international trade union federations who were forced to reform after the Cold War when their activities were hamstrung by ideological divisions; new social movement unions in Brazil, South Africa or Korea; new forms of labour organizations like homeworkers in India or African township traders; as well as labour-oriented grass roots groups and NGOs in various parts of the world. There has been a sea-change in labour movement attitudes; the functions of unions have been reconceptualized away from an economistic preoccupation with wages towards new notions of labour rights; and methods of organizing have become more like 'new' social movements. The Liverpool Dockers' strike is one example of the changing character of the labour movement. As Munck puts it, Labour is coming to be seen as just another movement or NGO.[52]

The 'new' anti-capitalist movement does include rejectionists and fundamentalists, who want to reverse globalization and return to a world of nation-states; an important tendency is the 'localizers' who want to return to small territorial communities.[53] It includes reformers who want to 'civilize' and 'democratize' globalization and offer concrete proposals like debt relief (Jubilee 2000) or a Tobin tax (ATTAC) to make this possible. And it includes those who want to abolish current global institutions and construct alternatives, like the Zapatistas' 'Declaration for Humanity and Against Neo-Liberalism'.[54] The opening offered by the Third Way politicians and, gingerly, by the international economic institutions at the end of the 1990s provided an opportunity to mobilize a movement whose demands go far beyond what any of the officials expected. The transformatory character of the movement's discourse, the involvement of women, workers and peasants in many parts of the world and the inclusion of social and economic rights in addition to the non-material concerns of the new social movements all mean that it has the potential to construct a genuinely popular form of action.

The demonstrations at the G8 summit in Genoa in 2001 seem to have marked a turning point. The demonstrations were marred by horrific violence, in which the anti-capitalist movement experienced its first martyr – a young man killed in the riots. The violence was partly initiated by a group known as the Black Box anarchists, and was partly a result of the aggressive behaviour of the Italian police, which was comparable, according to some of the protestors, to the behaviour of the police in Pinochet's Chile, who appeared to be in cahoots with the anarchists. But the Genoa Social Forum, as it was called, did come up with more concrete, sophisticated and better-formulated demands than many of the earlier 'parallel summits' and it seems to have provoked a serious response from global institutions and political elites. After Genoa, the IMF and World Bank responded to an invitation by Global Exchange, Jobs with Justice, 50 Years is Enough and Essential Action to engage in a public debate, writing that they were prepared to do so in principle, provided that it was a non-violent dialogue, conducted with respect for different views,[55] and Guy Verhofstadt, Prime Minister of Belgium and President of the European Union at the time, wrote an open letter to the so-called anti-globalization movement, published in many major newspapers around the world, and collected the responses in a book.[56] In France, the Health Minister, Bernard Kouchner, described the events at Genoa as a 'global kind of May 1968'. He anticipates a Tobin tax and global ethical investment. And the French Prime Minister, Lionel Jospin, welcomed 'the emergence of a citizens movement at the planetary level' and put forward an official proposal for a Tobin tax.[57]

The events of September 11, however, seemed to overwhelm the anti-capitalist movements and many planned activities were curtailed or postponed. But by early 2002, the movement had recovered. Some 50,000 people attended the World Social Forum in Porto Allegre in February, of which some 30,000 came from within Latin America, and some 300,000 demonstrated at the European Summit in Barcelona including parliamentarians and local officials. Some governments and international organizations have responded more positively to the anti-capitalist movement, out of a conviction that global redistribution may be an important factor in dealing with the causes of terrorism.

The role of the media

All the literature on social movements emphasizes the importance of forms of communication. The invention of the printing press is part of the explanation for the emergence of modern forms of protest. They were cosmopolitan because people became aware through newspapers of a wider community of people; they could relate not only to those they knew personally but also to fellow readers. Their protests were modular because others could easily learn their techniques and understand their demands through newspaper reports and the circulation of leaflets and petitions. They were autonomous because any individual could sign a petition or write to a newspaper. The 'imagined community' of nations was created by printing – the availability of novels and newspapers in the vernacular language, which allowed writers and readers to see themselves as part of a shared discourse.

The development of new forms of communication, based on the revolution in information technology as well as the spread of television and radio has created quite new 'imagined communities'. New social movements have capitalized on the possibility of what the French call *médiatique* events, something pioneered by Médecins sans Frontières. Both symbolic politics and information politics depend on instant news and images, especially through television, which makes possible the consciousness of a global community: 'Global political space is skimmed twenty-four hours a day and produced as a stream of televisual images featuring a terrorist attack here, a currency crisis there, and a natural disaster elsewhere. Global space becomes political space. Being there live is everything. The local is instantly global, the distant immediately closes. Place-specific struggles become global televisual experiences.'[58] One of the reasons why globalization makes closed totalitarian societies so difficult to sustain is the difficulty of insulating airwaves; thus East Europeans could watch West European television during the 1980s.

All the same, global networks like CNN and the BBC are only accessed by an English-speaking elite. Moreover, they do not only spread humanistic consciousness; they also spread awareness of the global consumer culture. State-run television or even radio in vernacular languages, on the other hand, can be used as a powerful propaganda tool for the 'new' nationalists, as was the case in the former Yugoslavia or 'hate radio' in Rwanda, which incited the genocide against Tutsis. Whereas newspapers mobilized a reading public, generally urban-based, television, radio and the circulation of videos operates as a form of rapid mobilization in remote areas where people do not have the reading habit, creating new 'imagined' communities based on fear and hate and reconstructions or reinventions of past grievances. Visual images and even voices are a much more powerful way to bring the past to life and to impose on the present real or imagined injustices of the past than history books and newspapers, although that happens too.

One of the positive developments of the 1990s has been the way in which democratization has led to the break-up of state monopolies in broadcasting. However, public service broadcasting has been difficult to foster and many of the new television and radio stations are largely entertainment driven. These private entertainment media can also provide mechanisms for the spread of particular versions of exclusive culture; in South Asia, the new satellite stations Zee TV and Star TV generate a kind of homogenized Hindu culture, based on Bollywood (Bombay-based Hindi films) and often expressing nationalistic bias in news reporting.

Nevertheless, the new openings have offered space to community groups, social movements and NGOs. A recent development has been the spread of community radio stations in Africa and especially in Latin America, often financed from abroad. The network of local independent radio stations, set up by radio B92 in Serbia, and financed by Western donors, is often considered the key factor in the fall of Milošević. The importance of community radio in Latin America may well explain the high density of global civil society activity as shown by statistics on numbers of INGOs and participation in parallel summits.[59] Another recent development has been the growing importance of talk shows, which it claimed is reinvigorating Africa's oral traditions.[60]

A fascinating phenomenon in the wake of September 11 is the Al Jazeera (the peninsular) TV station set up in Qatar and broadcasting in Arabic throughout the Middle East. Outspoken and independent, the station claims 35 million viewers and has been banned from Tunisia, Saudi Arabia and Morocco because of its criticisms of their regimes. Libya recalled its ambassador to Qatar and Jordan closed down its station bureau in Amman after criticism of the government.

Finally, of course, the Internet and email have become essential tools for organizing in the 1990s. Petitions are circulated through emails; networks are sustained through email lists; websites mobilize global demonstrations. And these are important tools for all categories of actors. Websites are as important for Diaspora groups as for INGOs.

Who is global civil society?

The different contemporary definitions of global civil society outlined in the first chapter tend to correspond to different categories of actors. Thus the neoliberal version of global civil society, where civil society is seen as a substitute for the state, a sort of laisser-faire politics, corresponds to the idea of a civil society composed of a market of NGOs. The very term NGO seems to imply 'not' or 'instead of' the state. The activist model of civil society corresponds to a civil society composed of social movements and civic networks, while the postmodern version would include the nationalist and fundamentalists as well.

At the end of the 1980s, the energies of the 'new' social movements culminated in the wave of democratization that affected not only Eastern Europe but also Africa, Asia and Latin America. I have described the dramatic growth of NGOs in part as the 'taming' of the new social movements in the aftermath of democratization and in response to new opportunities offered by international institutions, governments and even global companies. This was also a period when earlier social organizations and civic associations, often the legacy of 'old' social movements, were eroded and undermined by economic crisis and structural change. Thus in the 1990s, the sphere of informal politics came to be dominated, on the one hand, by NGOs and, on the other, by 'new' nationalist and fundamentalist movements.

This explains the growing disaffection with the term 'civil society', the criticism that has been increasingly levelled at the language of 'civil society' as being too Eurocentric and, indeed 'imperialistic'. Neera Chandhoke says that 'civil society' has become a hurrah word, emptied of content and 'flattened out'. 'Witness the tragedy that has visited proponents of the concept: people struggling against authoritarian regimes demanded civil society, what they got were NGOs... If everyone from trades unions, social movements, the UN, the IMF, lending agencies, to states both chauvinistic and democratic hail civil society as the most recent elixir to the ills of the contemporary world, there must be something wrong.'[61]

But that is perhaps precisely the advantage of the term. In the late 1990s, new grass roots groups and social organizations and the new anti-capitalist movement began to emerge, offering some renewed hope for creating an emancipatory economic and social agenda. If we think of global civil society, not as NGOs, but as a process through which contracts or agreements are negotiated at global, national and local levels, then it has to include all the various mechanisms through which individual voices can be heard. Civil society provides a legitimizing platform for discordant and radical demands – a name which explains why authorities have to take these demands seriously. Moreover, there are peace and human rights groups still struggling in oppressive regimes like Burma or Zimbabwe or in conflict zones like the Middle East, Kashmir, or the Caucasus, for whom the term 'global civil society' holds out some promise of being heard.

Global civil society includes the INGOs and the networks that are the 'tamed' successors to the new social movements of the 1970s and 1980s. It also includes the allies of transnational business who promote a market framework at a global level. It includes a new radical anti-capitalist movement which combines both the successors of the new social movements and a new type of labour movement. And to the extent that nationalist and fundamentalist movements are voluntary and participatory, i.e. they provide a mechanism through which individuals can gain access to centres of authority, then they have to be included as well; although in practice, as I have argued, in actually existing civil society, such distinctions may be difficult to draw. The array of organizations and groups through which individuals have a voice at global levels of decision-making represents a new form of global politics that parallels and supplements formal democracy at the national level. These new actors do not take decisions. Nor should they have a formal role in decision-making since they are voluntarily constituted and represent nobody but their own opinions. The point is rather that through access, openness and debate, policy-makers are more likely to act as a Hegelian universal class, in the interests of the human community.

The differentiated character of global civil society can be understood in terms of the complexity of the contemporary world. New Social Movement theorists sometimes talk about a 'movement society'.[62] The salient feature of globalization is the rapidity of technological and social change. The modern state, in its twentieth-century form, is too top heavy, slow and rigid to find ways of adapting to the myriad of unintended consequences of change. Civil society, a combination of different movements, NGOs and networks, is a way of expressing the reflexivity of the contemporary world.

It is the contestation between these different types of actors, as well as states, international institutions and transnational corporations that will determine the future direction of globalization. Will it be a 'civilizing' process in which global politics becomes the normal form of relations at a global level, or can we expect a return to inter-state relations, or, perhaps worse, a wild anarchic process involving inequality and violence? In the next chapter, I explore the changing patterns of governance and how they are related to changes in the character of warfare, as well as the influence of global civil society on these processes.

5
Globalization, the State and War

Critics of the concept of global civil society argue that civil society can only be understood within the context of a state. Since there is no global state, and indeed this would be undesirable, global civil society is a meaningless concept. And some would go further and argue that use of the term both undermines democracy at a national level and can be viewed as a form of imperialism. Those who favour the term, it is argued, make the misleading and potentially harmful claim that global civil society is a form of democracy at the international level, a way of representing the 'people' when this is clearly not the case.[1]

In this chapter, I argue that civil society needs governance, a framework of rules and institutions for managing society that civil society helps to construct and, at the same time, provides the conditions for civil society to function. Particularly important is the removal of fear, the absence of violence and coercion in everyday life so that people feel able to speak freely and be heard.

Historically the specific form of governance within which civil society developed was the centralized war-making territorial state and later, within the blocs, groups of centralized territorial war-making states. What this meant in practice was a profound limitation on the functioning of actually existing civil society. The rights and freedoms gained through popular struggles could always be withdrawn unilaterally in wartime. The universal values that were supposed to characterize civil society did not apply outside the borders of the state and hence actually existing civil society coexisted with conquest and expropriation of people living in other parts of the world. Freedom of association could be suppressed and civil society groups marginalized through the polarizing character of war and the disciplinary ideologies of the 'other'.

The advent of globalization gives rise to the possibility of a system of global governance, not a world state, but a framework of rules involving overlapping competencies among international organizations, local and regional government and states. Such a system of global governance is in the process of being constituted through negotiations and bargains which involve all these various organizations as well as global civil society. Such a system offers the possibility of going beyond the centralized war-making state and providing more not less space for civil society. Globalization does not mean the end of states but rather their transformation. One possibility is the transformation of states from being unilateralist war-making states to being multilateralist law-making states at global as well as national levels. The significance of 1989 was precisely the peaceful way in which the Cold War ended. It marked the historic possibility of moving beyond war between states or blocs.

In thinking about what this means for democracy, it is important to take into account, not just the formal procedures of democracy, for example, elections, important though these are, but also the substantive content of democracy, how citizens can directly influence the decisions that affect their lives. In the context of globalization, democracy, in a substantive sense, is undermined, however perfect the formal institutions, simply because so many important decisions that affect people's lives are no longer taken at the level of the state. There may be no formal way to rectify this situation since our network society contains few nodal decision points. But I will put forward the argument that a framework of global governance and an active global civil society at least offers some openings for participation at other levels.

The development of a system of global governance is by no means inevitable. Real reversals are possible. September 11, I would argue, represents one such reversal and will be discussed in the last chapter. In this chapter, I draw attention to conflicting tendencies, which are expressed in the new forms of warfare that characterize the post-1989 period, and put the case for a global security system based on humanitarian law, which could provide the basis for a framework of global governance. What became clear in the 1990s is that an effective civil society can only function in an atmosphere free of fear, even though there are always courageous groups and individuals who risk their lives for their causes, and that there have to be formal institutions at global, national and local levels who provide the conditions for security. I start with a few preliminary remarks about what is meant by 'global' and the changes in the character of global governance. I then consider the changing patterns of warfare and how they are related to the transformation of states. And in the last two sections, I discuss the possibilities for a humanitarian regime and what this might mean for the future of states and democracy.

Interpretations of the global

In the most popular usage, 'globalization' refers to the spread of global capitalism as well as to an array of policies (liberalization, deregulation and privatization) which facilitate this spread. Enthusiastic proponents of 'globalization' suggest that the spread of global capitalism is leading to a single global community and the demise of the nation-state.[2] No one disputes that this type of globalization has accelerated in the 1990s, as measured in trade or financial flows. Some argue, however, that these flows, as a share of national income, are no greater than they were before the First World War and that therefore this phase of globalization is reversible and that states remain powerful.[3] Others criticize the deterministic nature of this definition of 'globalization'. By reducing globalization to global capitalism, we concede the inexorable logic of market forces.

A second definition of 'globalization' is that to be found in much of the social science literature. This is the notion of globalization as growing interconnectedness in all fields – political, military, economic, cultural.[4] A version of this definition is 'time–space compression' or the 'stretching of social relations', that is to say, the notion that people's lives are increasingly influenced by events that take place far away.[5] An important element of this definition is the way in which changes in technology, especially increased air travel and new forms of information and communication technology, have led to the contraction of distance. Television allows us to become instantly aware of wars, disasters, coups or discoveries in different parts of the world. Air travel and the Internet create new horizontal communities of people, who perhaps have more in common than with those who live close by. According to Paul Virilio, 'now' has annihilated 'here' and has transformed the forms of social differentiation: 'The haves and the have-nots are then sorted out between those who live in the hyperreal shrunken world of instant communication, cyber-dynamics and electronic money transactions – and those, more disadvantaged than ever, who live in the real space of local villages, cut off from temporal forces that drive politics and economics.'[6]

According to this definition, it is growing political interconnect-edness, as expressed in the growth of international organizations, treaties, congresses and so on that is changing the character and role of states. Because of interconnectedness in all fields, states are losing their autonomy in making and enforcing rules; their power to shape regulatory frameworks and policies that affect their societies lies not so much in acting unilaterally as in their member-ship of various regional or global arrangements.

A third definition of globalization refers to the emergence of a common global consciousness. 'By global, we mean not just trans-formed concepts of time and space but the new social meanings that these have involved. I propose that we understand this as the development of a *common consciousness of human society on a world scale*. We mean an increasing awareness of the totality of human social relations as the largest constitutive framework of all relations. We mean that society is increasingly constituted primarily by this inclusive framework – rather than by distinct tribes, nations or religious communities although all of these remain in complex and overlapping ways within global society.'[7] This definition places more emphasis on human agency than the first or second defini-tions and defines the global as something more than spatial.

For proponents of this version of globalization, a key factor is the way in which global conflict has constructed a shared collec-tive memory. The wars of the twentieth century both denied and produced global consciousness. They were, at one and the same time, expressions of deep divisions within humanity and common moments that shaped the experiences and understanding of people all over the world, creating 'huge international and trans-national communities of struggle'.[8] Thus, for Robertson, who talks of the world as an 'imagined community', both the Holo-caust and Hiroshima were defining global events.[9] According to Shaw, even now, 'these experiences, as well as of new traumas which compound these lessons, are fuelling new developments of global law and morality'.[10] Thus the twentieth century is seen not just as a century of war but also a century in which there was a dramatic increase in 'peace oriented concepts and institutions'[11] as well in the development of human rights norms and machinery. The implication of this version of globalization is the possibility of a 'global state'[12] or, at least, a global rule of law.

What all three definitions share is the notion that globalization, however defined, has far-reaching implications for the nature of the state and indeed political power. For the first version, globalization involves the demise of the state; for the second, it involves the growing interconnectedness of state power and for the third, there exists the possibility of a global polity. In my view, this is why globalization talk has become so pervasive in the 1990s. Although the spread of global capitalism, growing interconnectedness and even global consciousness all began before 1989, it was the rupture in the nature of international political relations that took place as a result of the end of the Cold War which was so fundamental to the changes in the patterns of governance and which brought together and made more visible all these developments. Thus, for me, globalization is, at root, a political process, an outcome of deliberate human agency.

Although there have been globalizing political currents throughout history, a starting point for the current wave of globalization is the reactions against the state in the 1960s and 1970s. In the post-war period, the state was more interventionist than ever before, reaching out into nearly all aspects of everyday life not only in totalitarian societies but in the Atlantic region as well. The reactions to the state took two forms. One was the neoliberal reaction, the argument that state intervention in the economy had overreached itself and created rigidities that suppressed the market and militated against innovation and efficiency. Adherents of the free market came to power in Western Europe and North America in the 1980s and helped to provide the conditions for the accelerated spread of global capitalism. The other was the democratic reaction, the opposition to paternalism, authoritarianism and war described in the previous chapters. The new social movements that came into being in 1968 and after were to articulate a new form of radical democracy and a concern about global issues that was to inform the waves of democratization in southern Europe, Asia, Latin America, Africa and eventually Eastern Europe and was to provide the basis for global civil society.

Whereas the neoliberals were concerned to limit and roll back state power, at least in the economic arena, the new social movements were more concerned about accountability and participation.

Both political currents have contributed to an increased emphasis on individualism. Many theorists of globalization refer to growing individuation as part of the process.[13] The state, especially in the context of war, could be said to represent a collectivity; the inter-state system can be characterized as interactions between collectivities acting as individuals. Part of the difference between the domestic and the international, at least for those states that can be characterized as democratic, is the difference between an arena in which individuals are actors and an arena characterized by collective action. Hence one way of describing global politics is as an arena in which individuals as well as collectivities have an increasing possibility to participate. For the neoliberals, the emphasis on individuals was linked to private property, consumption and the pursuit of profit. For the new social movements, it was linked to life chances, human rights and political participation and the possibility of critical deliberation. Whereas the neoliberals were preoccupied with self-interest and greed as an equilibrating mechanism, the new social movements were concerned about moral autonomy and individual responsibility.

The revolutions of 1989 represented a turning point in the impact of these political currents on the pattern of governance. Already, individual states had been influenced both by neoliberalism and by democratization and already the autonomy, at least of smaller, weaker states, was being eroded. But 1989 marked the beginning of what might be called global civil society, that is to say, the moment when war and war-making started to become much less important in determining the relations between states and when individuals and citizens groups began to find genuine political openings at a global level.

Changes in the patterns of governance

Both global capitalism and global civil society have contributed to the growth of what David Held and his colleagues describe as growing political interconnectedness in the post-war period. Liberalization and deregulation at a national level, as Sol Picciotto points out, actually involves reregulation at a global level as trans-national companies attempt to create the conditions for a global market.[14] Pressure from social movements and NGOs, especially in the fields of human rights and the environment, have also promoted interconnectedness. Inter-governmental organizations, treaties, inter-governmental conferences, and diplomatic inter-connectedness, as Held et al. show, have all increased dramatically in the period after 1945.[15] What changed after 1989 was the opening up of both states and inter-governmental organizations to NGOs and other citizens groups operating in the global arena on a scale qualitatively different from what went before.

Those who are sceptical of the globalization thesis, in all its varieties, argue that states remain the primary agents for rule-making and rule enforcement. Inter-governmental organizations merely reflect the inter-state system, in which the primary actors are states. International NGOs may play a useful role but they are auxiliary to this system.[16] What this view misses is a fundamental change in the nature of the state, which appears to be coming to fruition in the post-Cold War period. And this has to do primarily with war-making capacity. As I have argued, the key characteristic of the modern state, which came into being somewhere between the fifteenth and eighteenth centuries, was its control of violence within a given territory. It was a 'coercion-wielding institution', as Tilly puts it,[17] or a 'bordered power container', in the words of Anthony Giddens.[18] Domestically, the modern state provided security for its citizens both through coercion and surveillance and through the extension of the rule of law. Internationally, the state defended its territory through war-making. The modern state emerged as part of an inter-state system in which sovereignty was mutually recognized and war, waged according to certain rules, could be justified in terms of a *raison d'état*. Interestingly, one of the foremost proponents of the concept of an international society of states, Robert Jackson, admits a fundamental change in this regard since the seventeenth and eighteenth centuries. 'Most noticeable is the absence of an expansive set of discretionary rights regarding the international use of armed force: the right of war and intervention, the right of conquest and the right of colonisa-tion.'[19] But he does not seem to grasp what this means for the very nature of governance. Bounded civil society depended on the existence of an 'other' even if there were different categories of 'other' – 'civilized' Europeans and 'less civilized' outsiders. The end of war as a unilateral option for state politics presupposes an acceptance of human equality; it eliminates the justification for the preservation of statist politics and the distinction between the inside and outside.

The growth of political interconnectedness cannot just be explained by new forms of communication or by the expansion of the global market.[20] It was always the case that growing interconnectedness in all fields depended on a degree of stability and, up to now, that has been provided by states. Thus the first wave of accelerated interconnectedness in the late nineteenth century depended on the stability provided by what Shaw calls the inter-imperial order. States controlled large swathes of territory and provided a framework within which international regulatory agencies could function; relations between empires were governed by a range of inter-governmental agreements. As in the subsequent Cold War period, the stability of the nineteenth century was largely confined to Western Europe. This was the period of brutal colonization, of genocide of native tribes in the Americas, of serfdom in Eastern Europe (up to the 1860s), and of slavery in Africa and the Americas. Moreover, the empires remained 'bordered power containers', and within the inter-imperial order, a devastating militarism developed in which popular nationalism was to combine with modern industry to produce the First World War and to destroy the achievements of nineteenth-century inter-governmentalism. As Shaw puts it:

> The realities of the national-international world order therefore belied the nineteenth century's pacific image. This was an era in which warfare was becoming more entrenched in state relations: not only in geopolitical rivalries, but the way in which state institutions organised economy and society. Military sectors became protected from market vagaries by ongoing state contracts: what would later be called the 'military-industrial complex', the centre of the modern war economy was born. Militarism grew as a social force, as mass armies trained the entire adult male populations of European states, at any one time, mobilising a substantial proportion as conscripts and the remainder as reservists. Militarism grew, too, as a cultural force, a source of many of the traditions, which were 'invented' in the imperial world.[21]

The second wave of accelerated interconnectedness took place after the Second World War. It was the Cold War Order, the bloc system, that was to provide the stability within which interconnectedness could develop. Again, it was a stability largely confined to Western Europe, North America, and Australasia; some 5 million people were killed in wars in every decade after the Second World War, largely in the so-called third world. Unlike the late nineteenth century, however, the bloc system represented a fundamental break with the inter-state system. The borders of violence were extended beyond the nation-state to cover groups of countries. It was blocs rather than states that became the 'bordered power containers'. The integration of military forces meant that members of blocs, with the exception of the dominant powers, no longer had the capacity to wage war unilaterally. Within the blocs, states had to find different ways of dealing with each other, even though the dominant powers, the United States and the Soviet Union, still retained their monopoly of violence and were able to use coercive methods against recalcitrant allies in the third world (in the case of both) and in Eastern Europe (in the case of the Soviet Union). The international became domesticated within the blocs. This provided the framework for the development of a system of multilateral agencies regulating global economic relations (the Bretton Woods system, the World Bank, or GATT) and, as I have argued, for the emergence of trans-European civil society at least in Western Europe.

Of course, the Cold War framework was a militaristic framework. Military spending, as a share of GNP, remained high, higher than in the pre-1914 period. Especially in the United States and the Soviet Union, the military industrial complex and the application of science and technology to armaments profoundly influenced economic development. Above all, the 'imaginary war' played out through nuclear deterrence, propaganda and spy stories provided the mechanism for justifying military spending and ensuring the social cohesion of the blocs. Individuals, groups and movements, as we saw in chapter 3, who challenged official positions could be marginalized (in the West) or repressed (in the East) as agents of the 'other'.

But the Cold War period ended not with a war as in 1914 but with the triumph, even if short-lived, of civil society. And this is why the end of the Cold War has opened up the possibility of extending the domestic beyond the boundaries of the blocs. A range of more extensive and intrusive arms control treaties, big reductions in military spending, the strengthening of

prohibitions against the use of force and of human rights legislation, the abandonment of conscription in many countries, offers a
real possibility of going beyond borders defined by violence.
Above all, the heritage of the new social movements in Europe
and North America, especially the anti-nuclear and Vietnam
movements, represented a serious constraint on war-making, on
the readiness to die for the state, what the Americans tend to
describe as the Vietnam syndrome. As Nigel Harris says of the
post-1968 movements: 'It is difficult to assess the impact of such a
relatively diffuse set of movements, but they began changes that
were to continue for a long time, creating societies that seemed far
remote from the old state form – above all, the granite inscrut-
ability of the male warrior began to disintegrate.'[22]

The end of an ideological confrontation linked to violence both
enhances the possibilities for cooperation in very concrete ways and
reduces the ability of officials to dismiss citizens' initiatives on
ideological grounds. 'With the breakdown of ideological and social
orthodoxy, the reluctance of many, perhaps most, diplomats and
UN practitioners to interact with non-governmental staff evaporated.'[23] Since authoritarian states could no longer be justified on
Cold War grounds, international institutions increasingly found it
necessary to support democracy and to find social partners in order
to implement international projects.[24] Essentially, the end of the
Cold War meant the possibility of greater cooperation between
international institutions and states, as well as individual participation as an alternative to collective discipline. In other words, the
end of the Cold War meant the possibility of global governance and
a system of international security based on law not war.

It should be stressed, however, that this is a possibility not yet a
reality – even though the conditions for a system of international
security are perhaps more favourable in the post-Cold War era
than ever before. Globalization, as I have argued, is a political
process involving profound changes in the patterns of governance.
The transformation of states from being centralized war-making
states to being the legitimate pillars of a system of global governance is but one tendency among others – a tendency that was
fostered beneath the structures of the Cold War and through the
activities of civil society groups. But there are, of course, other
possibilities and other tendencies and these are linked to the
changing character of warfare and to the different ways in which
states resist these developments. States are changing in a variety of

ways and these changes are bound up with changes in the types of
armed forces and the ways in which states perceive the future of
war. These conflicting tendencies need to be analysed and understood if the possibility of going beyond war is to have any prospect
of realization.

New forms of warfare

The end of the Cold War probably meant the end of wars of the
modern type – wars between states and groups of states, like
the World Wars or the Cold War, in which the aim, to quote
Clausewitz, was 'to compel an opponent to fulfil our will'. What
happened subsequently was not only a contraction of military
forces but also a restructuring and increased diversity of types of
military forces. There is a parallel with the pre-modern period,
which was also characterized by a diversity of military forces –
feudal levies, citizens, militias, mercenaries, pirates, for example –
and by a corresponding variety of types of warfare. In what
follows, I will describe how three main types of warfare are related
to different models of state transformations. These three types of
warfare correspond roughly to the ways in which certain types
of states have reacted to the post-Cold War context and have
resisted the renunciation of war-making. They are, of course,
overlapping and interacting, as I shall explain.

The first type of warfare can be described as *network warfare*;
armed networks of non-state and state actors. They include: paramilitary groups organized around a charismatic leader, warlords
who control particular areas, terrorist cells, fanatic volunteers like
the Mujahadeen, organized criminal groups, units of regular forces
or other security services, as well as mercenaries and private
military companies.

The form of warfare that is waged by these networks is to be
found in what I call 'new wars'.[25] The 'new' wars are not entirely
new, of course. In the form I describe them, they developed
before the end of the Cold War, especially in Africa. Moreover,
they have evolved out of the guerrilla and counter-insurgency
wars of an earlier period. This type of war became more visible
because of the end of the Cold War; but it is also the case that
these wars greatly increased in number during this period, and,
moreover, there was also a big increase in civilian suffering, as

measured by the ratio of military to civilian casualties and by the explosion of refugees and internally displaced persons.[26]

New wars, which take place in the Balkans, Africa, Central Asia and other places, are sometimes called internal or civil wars to distinguish them from intra-state or Clausewitzean war. I think this terminology is inappropriate for a number of reasons. First, the networks cross borders. One of the typical features of the 'new wars' is the key role played by Diaspora groups either far away (Sudanese or Palestinian workers in the Gulf states, former Yugoslav workers in Western Europe, immigrant groups in the new 'melting pot' nations like North America or Oceania) or in neighbouring states (Serbs in Croatia and Bosnia, Tutsis in Burundi or the DRC (Democratic Republic of Congo)). Secondly, the wars involve an array of global actors – foreign mercenaries and volunteers, Diaspora supporters, neighbouring states, not to mention the humanitarian actors such as aid agencies, NGOs or reporters.

And thirdly, and most importantly, the 'new wars' tend to be concentrated in areas where the modern state is unravelling and where the distinctions between internal and external, public and private, no longer have the same meaning. Such areas are characterized by what are called frail or failing states, quasi or shadow states. These are states, formally recognized by the outside world, with some of the trappings of statehood – an incomplete administrative apparatus, a flag, sometimes a currency – but where those trappings do not express control over territory and where access to the state apparatus is about private gain not public policy. In particular these are states where the monopoly of legitimate organized violence is being eroded.

Typically, these are formerly closed authoritarian states whose structures have resisted the impact of opening (both political and economic) to the outside world. In many of the areas where new wars take place, it is possible to observe a process that is almost the reverse of the process through which modern states were constructed as described by Tilly. Taxes fall because of declining investment and production, increased corruption and clientilism, or declining legitimacy. The declining tax revenue leads to growing dependence both on external sources and on private sources, through, for example, rent-seeking or criminal activities. Reductions in public expenditure as a result of the shrinking fiscal base as well as pressures from external donors for macroeconomic stabilization and liberalization (which also may reduce export revenues) further erode legitimacy. A growing informal economy associated with increased inequalities, unemployment and rural–urban migration, combined with the loss of legitimacy, weakens the rule of law and may lead to the re-emergence of privatized forms of violence: organized crime and the substitution of 'protection' for taxation; vigilantes; private security guards protecting economic facilities, especially international companies; or paramilitary groups associated with particular political factions. In particular, reductions in security expenditure, often encouraged by external donors for the best of motives, may lead to breakaway groups of redundant soldiers and policemen seeking alternative employment.

Of course, the networks that engage in new wars are not all to be found in these failing states. They include nodes in advanced industrial countries and, in the inner cities of the West, it is possible to observe gang warfare that has many of the characteristics of 'new wars'. Nevertheless, this type of state provides a fertile environment for this type of network.

Because networks are loose horizontal coalitions, unlike vertical disciplined armies of the past, a shared narrative, often based on a common identity, ethnic or religious, is an important organizing mechanism. What holds war-making networks together is generally an extreme political ideology linked to the nationalist and religious movements that I described in the previous chapter.

In these 'new wars', war itself is a form of political mobilization. In the typical wars of modernity, the aim was the military capture of territory and victory in battle. People were mobilized to participate in the war effort – to join the army or to produce weapons and uniforms. In the new wars, mobilizing people is the aim of the war effort; the point of the violence is not so much directed against the enemy; rather the aim is to expand the networks of extremism. Generally the aim is to control territory through political means, and military means are used to kill, expel or silence those who might challenge control. This is why the warring parties use techniques of terror, ethnic cleansing or genocide as deliberate war strategies. In the new wars, battles are rare and violence is directed against civilians. Violations of humanitarian and human rights law are not a side effect of war but the central methodology of new wars. Over 90 per cent of the casualties in the new wars are civilian and the number of refugees and displaced persons per conflict has risen steadily.

The strategy is to gain political power through sowing fear and hatred, to create a climate of terror, to eliminate moderate voices and to defeat tolerance. The political ideologies of exclusive nationalism or religious communalism are generated through violence. It is generally assumed that extreme ideologies, based on exclusive identities – Serb nationalism, for example, or fundamentalist Islam – are the cause of war. Rather, the spread and strengthening of these ideologies are the consequence of war. 'The war had to be so bloody', Bosnians will tell you, 'because we did not hate each other; we had to be taught to hate each other'.

The new wars generate a specific type of economy. Or to put it another way, these wars speed up the unravelling process described above and stimulate not a capitalist market but a new type of informally regulated economy based on violence. Because these networks flourish in states where systems of taxation have collapsed and where little new wealth is being created, and where the wars destroy physical infrastructure, cut off trade and create a climate of insecurity that prohibits investment, they have to seek alternative, exploitative forms of financing. They raise money through loot and plunder, through illegal trading in drugs, illegal immigrants, cigarettes and alcohol, through 'taxing' humanitarian assistance, through support from sympathetic states and through remittances from members of the networks. All of these types of economic activity are predatory and depend on an atmosphere of insecurity. Indeed, the new wars can be described as a central source of the globalized informal economy – the transnational criminal and semi-legal economy that represents the underside of globalization.

The logical conclusion that can be drawn from these three characteristics is that the new wars are very difficult to contain and very difficult to end. They spread through refugees and displaced persons, through criminal networks, and through the extremist viruses they nurture. We can observe growing clusters of warfare in Africa, the Middle East, Central Asia or the Caucasus. The wars represent a defeat for democratic politics, and each bout of warfare strengthens those with a vested political and economic interest in continued violence. There are no clear victories or defeats because the warring parties are sustained both politically and economically by continuing violence. The wars destroy what remains of productive activities, they undermine legitimacy, and they foster criminality. The areas where conflicts have lasted longest have generated cultures of violence, as in the jihad culture taught in religious schools in Pakistan and Afghanistan or among the Tamils of Sri Lanka, where young children are taught to be martyrs and where killing is understood as an offering to God, or in the combination of violence and magic in Africa.

It should be noted that there are other private or informal forces that do not correspond to this analysis. For example, in many of the new wars, villages or municipalities establish citizens' militias to defend local people – this was the case among some groups in Rwanda and also in Tuzla and Zenica during the Bosnian war. There are also more traditional guerrilla groups, whose strategy is to gain political control through winning hearts and minds rather than through sowing fear and hatred; hence they attack agents of the state and not civilians, at least in theory. Finally, there are numerous private-security companies, often established to protect multinational companies in difficult places, and mercenaries, who fight for money; tactics and forms of warfare, in these cases, depend largely on the paymasters.

A second type of warfare is what I call *spectacle warfare*.[27] Spectacle war is primarily undertaken by the United States, although the British war in the Falklands/Malvinas represented an anticipation of spectacle war although, unlike subsequent examples, troops were committed on the ground. Spectacle war involves war at long distance, using advanced aircraft and missile technology, or, in order to prevent own casualties, proxies like the KLA (Kosovo Liberation Army) in Kosovo or the Northern Alliance in Afghanistan. Spectacle war is the way the inherited structures of the Cold War period retain their power, in a context where American citizens no longer accept the conditions of an earlier national bargain, the readiness to die in war.

Although American military spending declined after 1989, it became much more technology-intensive.[28] Instead of ushering in a period of downsizing, disarmament and conversion (although some of that did take place at local levels in the USA), the end of the Cold War led to a feverish effort to apply information technology to military purposes, known as the Revolution in Military Affairs (RMA). The idea was to develop long-range weapons, guided by improved information, for precise and discriminate purposes in place of classic warfare. The cruise missile, the target of peace movement campaigns in the 1980s, can be described as the 'paradigmatic' weapon of RMA. It is a 'system that can be delivered by a variety of platforms (i.e. all three services can use it) and strike in a precise manner and with low collateral damage'.[29] It was the cruise missile that was used in the summer of 1998 against terrorist camps in Afghanistan and an alleged chemical weapons factory in Sudan after the bombings of the US embassies in Kenya and Uganda.

The Gulf War provided a model for what can be described as 'spectacle war'. It seemed to prove the argument that this high-tech warfare can be used against 'rogue states' sponsoring terror-ists. The same techniques were used against Iraq in December 1998, in Yugoslavia in 1999 and in Afghanistan in 2002. They satisfy a confluence of interests. They fulfil the needs of the scientists, engineers and companies that provide an infrastructure for the American military effort. They allow for a continuation of the imaginary war of the Cold War period from the point of view of Americans. They do not involve American casualties, and they can be watched on television and demonstrate the determination and power of the United States government – the 'spectacles' as Der Derian has put it, that 'serve to deny imperial decline'.[30] It is this imaginary character from an American perspective that explains Jean Baudrillard's famous remark that the Gulf War did not happen.

The programme for national missile defence (NMD) has to be understood in the same vein. NMD is an ambitious programme to knock out enemy missiles attacking the United States. Even if the system cannot work, it provides imaginary protection for the United States, allowing the United States to engage in casualty-free war without fear of retaliation. It provides the conditions for the Bush doctrine of pre-emption. This notion is evident from the way in which Donald Rumsfeld, the US Defence Secretary, talks about how NMD will enhance deterrence through a combination of defensive and offensive measures. The weakness of deterrence was always the problem of credibility, a problem that led to more and more usable nuclear weapons. With casualty-free war, the credibility of US action is more convincing; after all, it is said that the attack on the World Trade Towers was equivalent to the use of a sub-strategic nuclear weapon. NMD, at least psychologically, extends the possibilities for casualty-free war.

However, from the point of view of the victims, these wars are very real and not so different from new wars. However precise the strikes, it is impossible to avoid 'mistakes' or 'collateral damage'. It does not make civilian casualties any more palatable to be told they were not intended. Moreover, the destruction of physical infrastructure and the support for one side in the conflict, as in the case of proxies, results in many more indirect casualties. In the case of the Gulf War, direct Iraqi casualties can probably be numbered in the tens of thousands but the destruction of physical infrastructure and the ensuing wars with the Kurds and the Shi'ites caused hundreds and thousands of further casualties and seem to have entrenched the vicious and dangerous rule of Saddam Hussein. In the war in Afghanistan, there were around 1,000–1,300 civilian casualties from 'collateral damage' but thousands more died as a consequence of the worsening humanitarian crisis and some 500,000 people fled from their homes; in addition it is estimated that some 4,000 Taliban and al-Qaeda troops were killed.[31] Even more importantly, it is impossible to control the situation on the ground from the air. Nothing can be done to stop escalating new wars as against civilians, as happened in Kosovo during the bombing of Yugoslavia. Far from extending support for democratic values, casualty-free war shows that American lives are privileged over the lives of others and contributes to a perception of the United States as a global bully.

Terms like imperialism are, however, misleading. The United States is best characterized not as an imperial power but as the 'last nation-state' or, as Javier Solana, the Secretary General of the European Council, has put it, a 'global unilateralist'. It is the only state, in this globalized world, that still has the capacity to act unilaterally. Its behaviour is determined less by imperial considerations than by concerns about its own domestic public opinion. Casualty-free war is also in a sense a form of political mobilization. It is about satisfying various domestic constituencies, not about influencing the rest of the world, even though such actions have a profound impact on the rest of the world.

Martin Shaw uses the term 'risk-transfer war' to describe this kind of war. He argues that these are wars where the risk is transferred to local allies on the ground and to enemy forces and civilians.[32] According to Shaw, risk-transfer war tends to involve high enemy military casualties, small 'accidental' massacres of civilians, some 50–100 in each case as a result of 'mistakes' or 'collateral damage', and high indirect civilian casualties because of the disruption of war. Media management is a critical component of risk-transfer war so as to minimize the impact on public opinion of the 'accidental' massacres. My analysis does not substantially differ, but the term 'spectacle war' emphasizes the function of war as a form of political legitimation, an ideology, in a context where citizens are no longer ready to sacrifice their lives and governments are no longer ready to guarantee the full range of rights.

The third type of warfare can be described as *neo-modern warfare*. Neo-modern warfare refers to the evolution of classical military forces in large transition states. These are states that are undergoing a transition from a centralized economy to a more internationally open market-oriented system and, yet, which are large enough to retain a sizeable state sector and to prevent unravelling. Typical examples are Russia, India and China. They are not large enough to challenge the USA and they are constrained by many of the imperatives of globalization, subject to many of the pressures that are experienced by frail or failing states. They tend to adopt extreme ideologies that resemble the ideologies of the 'new wars' – Russian or Hindu chauvinism, for example. And there are often direct links to and even cooperation with the shadier networks, especially in Russia. Israel should probably also be included in this category, although its capacity to retain a sizeable military sector is due less to its size than to its dependence on the United States.

These states have retained their military forces, including nuclear weapons. In the case of India, there has been a significant increase in military spending throughout the 1990s and it could be argued that term 'arms race' could be applied to India and Pakistan, especially after the 1998 nuclear tests. Pakistan, however, could be said to be closer to the networks of the new wars with its links to militants in Kashmir and Afghanistan; in other words somewhere between network warfare and neo-modern warfare, as was the case for Serbia during the wars in former Yugoslavia. In the case of Russia, there was a dramatic contraction of military spending after the break-up of the Soviet Union and a deep crisis in the military-industrial complex. But pressure to increase military spending has increased and the demands of the war in Chechnya is leading to a reassessment of the relative importance of conventional versus nuclear weapons. The proposed cuts in nuclear weapons agreed between Putin and Bush are supposed to release funds for conventional improvements. China is also engaged in military expansion especially since 1998, when the military were prohibited from engaging in commercial activities. Given the reductions in Russian nuclear capabilities and the new generation of Chinese systems, China will come to look more like a competitor to Russia, especially in the nuclear field.

Neo-modern warfare is either limited inter-state warfare or counter-insurgency. These states envisage wars on the classic Clausewitzean model. They engage in counter-insurgency in order to defeat extremist networks as in Chechnya or Kashmir. Or they prepare for the defence of borders against other states, as in the case of the Kargil war between India and Pakistan in 1998. Unlike the United States, these states are prepared to risk casualties and, in the case of the Chechen war, Russian casualties have been extremely high. The typical tactics used against the networks are shelling from tanks, helicopters or artillery, as well as population displacement to 'clean' areas of extremists or 'terrorists'. The impact on civilians is thus very similar to the impact of the 'new wars'. Yet precisely because of the growing destructiveness of all types of weapons, military victory against an armed opponent is very difficult. Grozny has virtually been reduced to rubble. Yet still resistance persists.

The networks have understood that they cannot take territory militarily, only through political means, and the point of the violence is to contribute to those political means. The states engaged in neo-modern warfare are still under the illusion that they can win militarily. The consequence is either self-imposed limits, as in the case of inter-state war, or exacerbation of 'new wars' as in the case of Kashmir, Chechnya or Palestine, where counter-insurgency merely contributes to the political polarizing process of fear and hate. In other words, the utility of modern military force, the ability to 'compel an opponent to fulfil our will', is nowadays open to question.

Thus it can be concluded that all three types of armed forces (the networks, the new American military forces, and the neo-modern military forces) engage in wars with very similar consequences – indiscriminate suffering for civilians (even though the Americans claim that their greater precision and discriminateness minimizes such suffering). None of these wars is able to solve conflicts. The Americans did succeed in liberating Kosovo and overthrowing the Taliban in Afghanistan but these were very special circumstances in which an extraordinarily expensive and powerful effort was expended against rather weak enemies and they did leave many issues unresolved. What these wars do, however, is strengthen extremists on all sides, weaken civil society and create a criminalized economy. Nowadays, therefore, the emphasis of those who are concerned about such suffering has to be directly with the ways to control war.

The humanitarian alternative

Perhaps the most hopeful approach to the contemporary problem of controlling war, today, is through the extension and application of international humanitarian law (the 'laws of war') and human rights law. During the 1990s, much greater importance was accorded to humanitarian norms – the notion that the international community has a duty to prevent genocide, violations of humanitarian law (war crimes) and massive violations of human rights (crimes against humanity). The idea of overriding state sovereignty in the case of humanitarian crises became much more widely accepted. The establishment of the Yugoslav and Rwanda Tribunals paved the way for the establishment of an International Criminal Court. The Pinochet and Ariel Sharon cases called into question the principle of sovereign immunity.

Humanitarian law is not, of course, new. Its origins lie in the codification of 'laws of war', especially under the auspices of the International Red Cross, in the late nineteenth century. The aim was to limit what we now call 'collateral damage' or the side effects of war, above all to prevent the indiscriminate suffering of civilians, and to ensure humane treatment for the wounded and for prisoners of war. These laws codified rules in Europe which dated back to the Middle Ages and underlay a notion of 'civilized' warfare, which was important in order to define the role of the soldier as the legitimate agent of the state, as a hero not a criminal. (Of course, these rules were not applied outside Europe against 'barbarians' or the 'rude nations'.) And in the post-1945 period, a range of human rights legislation was also introduced.

Several factors, however, led to this renewed emphasis on humanitarian law in the last decade. One factor has been the change in the nature of warfare, even though some aspects were presaged in the holocaust and the bombing of civilians in the Second World War. As argued above, violations of humanitarian law and human rights law are no longer 'side effects' of war; they

represent the core of the new warfare. Therefore taking humanitarian law seriously is one way of controlling the new warfare.
A second factor was, of course, the post-Cold War global context.
The end of the Cold War provided an opportunity, for the first
time, for concerted international action. It also allowed the 'new
wars' to become more visible and for the new global discourse,
drawn from the dialogue of the 1980s, about humanitarianism and
human rights to supplant the language of the Cold War.

And a third factor was the emergence of global civil society, as
evidenced by the growth of humanitarian and human rights
NGOs. Both types of NGOs reflected a growing consciousness
of a set of duties towards mankind, which developed as a consequence of the experience of the wars in the twentieth century –
something that was part of the new mood of questioning which
followed the events in 1968. For humanitarian NGOs, the war in
Nigeria in 1969 was a turning point. It was the moment when the
International Committee of the Red Cross (ICRC) abandoned its
insistence on neutrality and operating within the framework of
consent. The ICRC was conscious that its insistence on neutrality
had prevented the ICRC from publicly protesting about what it
knew to be happening to the Jews in the Second World War and
there were fears of genocide in Biafra. Thus the ICRC, together
with more recent humanitarian NGOs influenced by the student
movements of the 1960s and the interrogations about the Second
World War, decided to organize an airlift to Biafra without the
consent of the Nigerian authorities.

For many of the newer NGOs that emerged out of the post-1968
ferment, Biafra was the defining moment. Bernard Kouchner, for
example, who had been a student in Paris in 1968, was working for
the International Red Cross in Nigeria. He was shocked by the
unwillingness of the ICRC to speak out about what was happening,
bringing back echoes of the silence of the ICRC in the Second
World War.[33] 'By keeping silent, we doctors were accomplices in
the systematic massacre of a population.'[34] Kouchner started the
International Committee Against Genocide in Biafra and started to
use the media to publicize what was happening. 'We were using the
media before it became fashionable. . . . We refused to allow sick
people and doctors to be massacred in silence and submission.'[35] In
1971, he was to found Médecins sans Frontières (MSF).

Subsequently, many of the groups formed or shaped by that
experience went on to respond to crises in various parts of the

world – earthquakes, floods, famines and war. In 1984, the famine in Ethiopia sparked a debate about humanitarianism and political action, about whether humanitarians can be neutral or whether it is necessary to take sides.[36] By the mid-1980s, this new type of war had become increasingly important. In Mozambique or Afghanistan, official agencies increasingly began to see the advantage of NGOs as a form of non-governmental intervention and a way of working in war zones without permission. In several places, 'corridors of tranquillity' or 'humanitarian corridors' were established to provide relief. Operation LifeLine in Sudan was another particularly important episode where many of these techniques were developed, particularly through UNICEF and its programmes for immunization of children. It was then that 'clamours for more muscular support' began to be raised.[37]

This was the period that Bernard Kouchner, together with his colleague, the lawyer Mario Bettani, launched the idea of a Devoir d'Ingérence (Duty to Interfere), which later became a Droit d'Ingérence (Right/Law of Interference). Kouchner became French Minister of Humanitarian Action in 1988, and the same year, the United Nations General Assembly passed the resolution 43/131, which put these arrangements on a more formal footing. The resolution reaffirmed the sovereignty of states but recognized that the 'international community makes an important contribution to the sustenance and protection' of victims in emergency situations. Failure to provide humanitarian assistance 'constitutes a threat to life and human dignity'. The resolution stressed the 'important contribution' of 'intergovernmental and non-governmental organisations working with strictly humanitarian motives'. Subsequently, General Assembly Resolution 45/100 praised the Secretary-General for continuing consultations on the establishment of 'humanitarian corridors'.[38]

The emergence of pro-democracy and human rights movements in the third world and Eastern Europe, as described in chapter 3, was also very important in changing consciousness. In Europe and North America, the new social movements which evolved after the 1960s spawned human rights groups sometimes in dispute with the traditional left. In the United States, it was the coup in Chile and the growth of human rights groups in Latin America during the 1970s and 1980s that led to the emergence of transnational human rights networks.[39] In France, the debate about *tiermondisme* led many French intellectuals to attack the simplicities

of those traditional left groups who had unquestioningly supported liberation movements in the third world and to place
increasing emphasis on democratic freedoms and human rights;
the group Libertés sans Frontières was an expression of this line of
thought. In the rest of Europe, the mass peace movement of the
1980s stimulated the debate about human rights and the relation
of peace to justice.

The 1989 revolutions gave further impetus to the human
rights movements. Particularly important was the war in Bosnia-
Hercegovina. In Europe, a mass movement developed in the wake
of the war, to a large extent based on the movements that had
been active in the 1980s. Within the former Yugoslavia, various
pro-democracy groups had sprung up during the late 1980s and
had made links with the groups involved in 'détente from below'.
They saw the war as an attack on democracy and civil society;
indeed the term civic or even democratic came to mean non-
nationalist. In 1991–2, they mobilized support across Europe to
try to prevent war. For example, they organized a peace caravan in
September 1991. Some forty European activists travelled by bus
through Slovenia, Croatia, Serbia and Bosnia, making links with
local anti-war activists. The caravan culminated in Sarajevo,
where a human chain of 10,000 people linked the mosque, the
synagogue, the Orthodox and Catholic Churches. It is often not
known that the war in Bosnia began when snipers attacked a
demonstration of some 200,000 people calling for peace and
international intervention.

After the war began, hundreds of groups sprang up both to collect
and distribute aid and to increase awareness and make protests. In
Italy, for example, the Italian Consortium for Solidarity was established in 1993 linking civil society groups and organizations. From
Italy alone, more than 15,000 volunteers travelled to the war zones
and some 2,200 convoys were organized. But throughout Europe
similar mobilizations took place, including the new democratic
countries of Central Europe. In the Czech Republic, for example,
the People in Need Foundation (Clovek v Tisni) ran a television
campaign and even persuaded army officers to donate part of their
salary. A particularly interesting group was Workers' Aid for Tuzla,
which later became International Workers' Aid. This group was
started by British miners who had received support from the town
of Tuzla during the 1984 miners' strike and wanted to repay their
debt. Those who drove convoys or established local offices in war

zones did risk their lives and a number of volunteers were killed from several European countries. As well as grass roots groups, intellectuals and cultural figures (artists, writers, actors and actresses) played an important role in the movement, especially in France, the United States and Central Europe.

What they learned in this period was that civil society mobilization was not enough. Civil society needs a framework of security; hence the growing pressure for an international framework of law to be applied in local situations where the state unravels. Public pressure led to a series of interventions by the international community – the protection of aid convoys and the establishment of humanitarian corridors, the establishment of safe havens and of a no-fly zone, the setting up of a tribunal for war crimes committed in the former Yugoslavia, the establishment of international administrations for Sarajevo and Mostar. In retrospect, the latter two innovations were to have considerable significance. The setting up of the Hague Tribunals created a momentum for an International Criminal Court and the demand for the arrest of war criminals raised the issue of international law enforcement. Likewise the establishment of international administrations paved the way for the protectorates that were established in Bosnia and Kosovo.

By the end of the 1990s, it could be said that pressure from global civil society had given rise to widespread acceptance of humanitarian norms. As Human Rights Watch put it, in their World Report for the year 2000:

> The progress made . . . in standing up to crimes against humanity represents more than a doctrinal qualification of the prerogatives of sovereignty. Behind the advances in international justice and the increased deployment of troops to stop atrocities lies an evolution in public morality. More than at any time in recent history, the people of the world today are unwilling to tolerate severe human rights abuses and insistent that something be done to stop them. This growing intolerance of inhumanity can hardly promise an end to the atrocities that have plagued so much of the twentieth century. Some situations will be too complex or difficult for easy outside influence. But this reinforced public morality does erect an obstacle that, at least in some cases, can prevent or stop these crimes and save lives.[40]

Nevertheless, in Bosnia, as in other interventions, there was no consensus about how to intervene in support of humanitarian norms. The actual experience of intervention has been disappointing and in some cases shameful. In July 1995, Dutch peacekeepers handed over the 8,000 men and boys of the UN-declared safe haven of Srebrenica to Serb forces and they were all massacred. In Rwanda, UN forces were withdrawn just as the genocide of 800,000 Tutsis began, despite the impassioned plea of the Canadian UN Commander, General Dallaire, to establish safe havens. In Somalia, where the United States led a peacekeeping operation aimed at delivering humanitarian assistance, which failed to disarm militia and bring some semblance of security, peacekeeping forces were withdrawn after American soldiers were killed and their mutilated bodies publicly paraded in front of television cameras. Indeed, it is hard to find a single example of humanitarian intervention during the 1990s that can be unequivocally declared a success. Especially after Kosovo, the debate about whether human rights can be enforced through military means became ever more intense.

Some argue that intervention has to take the form of 'spectacle war' as was the case in Kosovo, since outside states would never risk casualties among their own citizens in faraway places. This argument gained momentum in the context of the war in Afghanistan, where it is argued that the effectiveness of 'spectacle war' was clearly established. Others claim that the Kosovo example shows that military intervention is wrong; human rights groups have contributed to a new 'military humanism' or 'human rights imperialism' that legitimizes a new American 'colonising enterprise'[41] and this argument also seems to have been given substance by the Afghan war. They do not believe that governments, whose job is to protect the 'national interest', can act for 'noble purposes'. They suggest that humanitarian intervention should only be undertaken by NGOs. The task of human rights protection, the delivery of relief or conflict prevention and resolution, according to this view, should be undertaken by civil society, not governments.

The risk is that both these positions could end up prolonging war perhaps indefinitely. Air strikes and overwhelming force tend to reinforce particularist views of the world and can contribute to polarization and destabilization, while giving the impression of action. It is true that the air strikes against Yugoslavia did, in the end, lead to the liberation of Kosovo. But they also provided a cover under which Milošević could accelerate ethnic cleansing of

Albanians from Kosovo and, consequently, when the Albanians returned to Kosovo, ethnic cleansing against Serbs took place as well. Moreover, the experiences of neo-modern warfare suggest that ground attacks are not much more effective; they cannot restore order. At the same time, however, the anti-military humanitarian position may alleviate hunger and even sometimes protect people, but, by being ineffective, too even-handed and sometimes vulnerable, it cannot stop genocide and it risks discrediting the non-violent civil society position.

There is a third position, especially among those groups that were active in the Cold War period, and this is one that distinguishes humanitarian intervention from war. Humanitarian intervention is a method for enforcing international law with respect to human rights and the laws of war, in situations where the state has collapsed or where the state itself violates the law. Law enforcement is different from war fighting. It involves a minimization of casualties on all sides, direct protection of the victims and the arrest of war criminals. It scrupulously respects human rights and humanitarian law in the implementation of its mission. It is more like policing than war fighting although it may require more robust action than domestic policing. It involves impartiality in the sense that all civilians, whatever their views or ethnic background, need to be protected and likewise all war criminals need to be opposed whatever side they are on. But this is not the same as neutrality since it is nearly always the case that one side is more responsible for human rights abuses than the other. The war in Kosovo, justifiable or not, cannot be classified as a humanitarian intervention since this was a war between Nato and Yugoslavia rather than a direct intervention to protect Kosovar Albanians on the ground.

A number of recent reports have emphasized that the new role of international peacekeeping is a form of policing. First and foremost, its job is to protect civilians since they are the main targets of the new wars.[42] The new peacekeeping is seen as somewhere between traditional peacekeeping (separating sides) and peace enforcement (taking sides). Outright military victory is *very* difficult nowadays, at least if we are unwilling to contemplate mass destruction. The aim of humanitarian intervention is not to defeat an enemy but to protect civilians and stabilize war situations so that non-extremist tolerant politics has space to develop. Techniques like safe havens or humanitarian corridors are ways of protecting civilians and also increasing the international presence on the ground so as to influence political outcomes. These have to be part of a package of other measures that include material assistance, negotiations, and support for civil society, which can be applied as prevention and reconstruction measures as well during conflict.

This position is consistent with the idea that civil society has an important humanitarian role to play in conflicts. But civil society can only be sustained in the framework of a rule of law. This is the lesson that was rudely learned at the outbreak of the Bosnian war, when, in the euphoric aftermath of the 1989 revolutions, it was hoped that citizens could prevent war through mass public action. Moreover, the effect of new wars, and Bosnia is a good example of this, is to destroy civil society. Because new wars represent a form of political mobilization, extremists are generally strengthened in war and civil society greatly weakened.

The version of humanitarian intervention as international law enforcement is situated in the middle ground between inaction and spectacle war. Up to now, no international military operation can be easily categorized as fitting this description of humanitarian intervention. Does this mean that the idea of humanitarian intervention as international law enforcement is utopian? It is certainly true that neither the legal system nor the structure and training of military forces is yet adapted to what might be described as 'robust' law enforcement. But those who favour a security system based on international law enforcement would argue that this has to be done. The world can no longer stand aside when genocide is committed or, at best, feed the victims. Spectacle war can have the opposite effect from that intended by engaging in forms of violence that are not so very different from the forms of violence they are supposed to prevent; there is no such thing as a 'civilized' war any longer, if there ever was.

For such an approach to work, there needs to be a much more substantial commitment than displayed hitherto – a commitment that goes beyond rhetoric. In part, it is a commitment to resources. The term humanitarian intervention perhaps needs to be reconceptualized as international presence in conflict-prone areas – a presence that represents a continuum from civil society actors, to international agencies, up to and including international peacekeeping troops on a much larger scale than up to now. In part, it means a change in outlook, especially the training, equipment, principles and tactics of peacekeeping troops. But, above all, it involves a genuine belief in the equality of all human beings and this entails a readiness to risk the lives of peacekeeping troops to save the lives of others, where this is necessary. It should be stressed that I am not talking about full-scale war and, therefore, the risks are less than in a conventional ground war. But even in the most well-ordered societies, police take risks to maintain the security of ordinary citizens, as do fire fighters, for example. The human rights enforcement position would require the same sort of commitment at an international level.

The legitimacy of political institutions, as I have argued in chapter 2, is intimately linked to the physical protection of citizens. The new types of warfare can be viewed as 'protection-failures'.[43] How and whether this protection is provided will shape the future of political institutions, whether it is possible to reconstitute a social contract at a global level. Can there be a global social contract which would guarantee the implementation of fundamental human rights? Does this imply that the individual has to be prepared to pay global taxes or, more importantly, does the individual have to be prepared to die for humanity? I think the individual has to be prepared to risk life for humanity but not in an unlimited way (as was the case with statist wars) since he or she is part of humanity. Humanitarian intervention is less risky than neo-modern warfare although more risky than spectacle war or traditional peacekeeping. Indeed, human rights activists and aid workers already risk their lives for humanity. It is sometimes said that this notion is ridiculously utopian – dying for hearth and home is quite different from risking life for something as grand and abstract as humanity. But risking life for one's nation is in fact a relatively recent invention. The notion that there is some higher good beyond secular notions of nation and state long preceded this invention.

Multilateralism and democracy

Robert Cooper suggests that 1989 marks a change in the nature of the international states system as profound as the Treaty of Westphalia in 1648, which is usually considered to represent the beginning of a states system.[44] He describes the emergence of what he calls postmodern states in the aftermath of the Cold War.

Postmodern states are states which 'are no longer governed by the territorial imperative'.[45] They are embedded in an international framework, in which the distinction between domestic and international has been eroded, where borders matter less, where there is mutual interference and surveillance in domestic affairs, where force is prohibited and where security is based on 'transparency, mutual openness, interdependence and mutual vulnerability'.[46] Postmodern states abide by the rules they have established not because there is a collective enforcement mechanism but because of 'their individual interest in maintaining the collective system'.[47] In postmodern states, the individual becomes much more important and concepts like 'raison d'etat and the amorality of Machiavelli have been replaced by a moral consciousness that applies to international relations as well as domestic affairs'.[48]

Robert Cooper's postmodern states are what I would call multilateral states. They are close to what Ian Clark calls 'globalised' states[49] and what Ulrich Beck calls 'cosmopolitan' or post-national states.[50] By multilateral, I mean states that see their primary interest as a multilateral framework of rules, a system of global governance. The legitimacy of such a system derives from states; they remain the units that are legally constituted to construct international organizations, sign and ratify treaties, or vote in various international fora. Multilateral states remain the juridical repository of sovereignty, even if their ability to make and enforce rules cannot be exercised unilaterally but depends on participation in an interconnected system. They remain coercion-wielding institutions, responsible for domestic policing and control of the military. But their domestic control of violence is, as it were, supervised, in the context of a new array of international human rights instruments, and the external use of force can only be legitimated through an international process. At the heart of such a system of rules is a humanitarian regime that aims to guarantee physical security for individuals all over the world, in other words, that has the capacity to uphold human rights in practice when states fail to do so.

Philip Bobbitt, in a highly acclaimed book about war, law and the state, suggests that the nation-state is being supplanted by the market state, which is no longer able to sustain the national compacts of earlier eras in the context of the global marketplace.[51] He distinguishes three types of market states: the entrepreneurial state, which justifies military intervention in the

domestic affairs of others according to its own criteria of legitimacy; the managerial state, which insists on international
legitimacy and multilateral arrangements; and the mercantile
state, which opposes intervention in the name of sovereignty.
Thus the entrepreneurial state seems to be the United States and
possibly Britain, the supporters of spectacle war. The managerial
state is what I call a multilateralist state, and the mercantile state is
the transition state, the upholders of neo-modern militarism.

Typical multilateral states are to be found in Europe, Canada,
Japan, South Africa, or in Latin America. There is evidence to
suggest a strong correlation between the degree of globalization
(the extent of interconnectedness of trade, capital, people and
organizations), multilateralism (signing and ratifying treaties,
respecting international rules, joining international organizations)
and the density of global civil society (membership in INGOs,
hosting parallel summits, tolerating strangers).[52] The causal
relationships that might explain this correlation have not yet
been investigated. But it is possible to speculate that the more a
society is integrated into the world economy and society, the
greater its interest in multilateralism. The more multilateral the
state, then the more it is likely to provide access to and funding for
global civil society groups as a way of strengthening support for
multilateralism. And the more a society is globalized and the
more multilateral the government, the more favourable is the
infrastructure and the opportunity for the growth of global civil
society. And, in a virtuous circle, global civil society itself
contributes to interconnectedness and presses government in
multilateral directions. In other words, all three phenomena feed
off each other.

This analysis raises two further questions. One has to do with
the possibility of global multilateralism, and the other has to do
with democracy. Robert Cooper's terminology implies a teleological view of history, in which pre-modern states (which he
sees as failed or collapsing states) and modern states (which
I would call unilateral states) are progressing towards a postmodern goal. But what if this is not the case? What if unilateralism
and state failure are alternative ways of adapting to globalization?
Is multilateralism a new form of free trade imperialism, like
Britain in the mid-nineteenth century? And are unilateralism and
multilateralism doomed to coexist like the coexistence of civil
and 'uncivil' societies in the era of bounded civil society?

In my view, unilateralism and state failure are alternative ways of reacting to globalization but, unlike previous eras when the world was divided into 'civil' and 'uncivil zones', I do not believe that the coexistence of multilateralism and unilateralism can be sustained. This is because of interconnectedness and because of the changed nature of warfare. On the one hand, unilateral war-making cannot provide a basis for security, as I have argued above; it can only lead to more war. It can sustain bellicose political leaders but it cannot provide individual security. On the other hand, unilateralism cannot prevent the extension of global civil society and domestic challenges to war-making. This does not mean that multilateralism represents the future, that war-making can be controlled through domestic pressure, although this is a necessary element in any humanitarian regime. What it means is the likelihood of struggle, in which extremist leaders use the instrument of war not to defeat an enemy but to suppress domestic critics. What it means is that continued unilateralism could squeeze multilateralism and also global civil society, leading to a violent world, the 'outside' of war and anarchy moving 'inside' rather than the other way round. Whether the multilateralists can succeed in moving beyond war, in moving the 'inside' to the 'outside', will depend both on the strength of global civil society and on the readiness to construct an effective humanitarian regime.

In other words, a multilateral regime has to be constructed on the basis of a new bargain, in which multilateral states agree to provide resources and peacekeeping troops to protect citizens and to uphold international law, and in which citizens accept the obligation to pay for and to be involved in humanitarian missions.

Neither a reversion to unilateralism nor a multilateral regime offers much hope for the future of democracy, as we have conceived it in the past. Multilateral states remain the sites of formal representative democracy although the national bargains of an earlier period are 'hollowed out'. The demands of those who reinvented civil society in the 1980s were for a radical extension of democracy. They wanted democracy in a substantive sense, meaning political equality, empowerment and the ability to influence the decisions that affect your life.[53] The 1980s and 1990s witnessed the spread of formal democracy and, at the same time, increased disenchantment with the formal political process giving rise to growing apathy and frustration. The paradox is explained

by the erosion of the national bargain – the decline in commitment on both sides, citizens and state. Loyalty to the state and
readiness to go to war and pay taxes has declined alongside the
willingness and ability of the state to secure economic and social
rights or political rights in a substantive sense. The interconnectedness of decision-making has meant the 'hollowing out' of
democracy – democracy has become 'management', according to
Robert Cox.[54] In multilateral states, the primary task of voters is
to elect legitimate actors on the global stage, actors who will
pursue political programmes at a global level. Since political
culture, in most countries, remains focused on domestic issues,
electorates have, by and large, not come to terms with their
changed role.

Unilateralism, however, cannot reverse this 'hollowing out' of
formal procedural democracy. On the contrary, unilateralism is
likely to be associated with ideologies of the 'other' and intrusive
legislation justified in the name of 'national security'.

Is the implication of this argument that democracy has to be
reconstituted at the global level? I am sceptical about this possibility, even though I favour proposals for, say, a global parliament.[55] This is not the place to discuss the various obstacles to
global representative democracy; they include the risks of major-
itarianism, the problems of distance, and the complexity of contemporary society. But the question arises as to whether global
civil society can act as what Rosenau calls a 'functional equivalent'
to democracy.[56] Can global civil society both push for the construction of global governance and at the same time act as a form
of oversight preventing abuses of power by the newly created
institutions, as was the case in the formations of states? Can global
civil society provide a mechanism through which individuals, if
they choose, are able to participate at a global level and through
which they can enhance the prospects of influencing the decisions
that they care about?

Global civil society cannot claim to 'represent' the people in the
way that formally elected states can and do. But the issue is less
one of representation than of deliberation. Parliamentary democracy was always about deliberation. The idea was not to mandate
members of parliament but rather to vote for individuals who
could be trusted to debate and deliberate issues in an honest way
in the public interest. That idea has been undermined in a national
context for a variety of reasons, including media sloganizing and

party discipline. But one important reason is the complexity and rapid changes of modern life and the need for specialized knowledge. By specialized knowledge, I do not mean the knowledge of the supposedly objective scientist or technician, I mean the knowledge of people who are deeply engaged in particular issues and who have thought about solutions from different points of view.

What we are seeing within the emerging framework of global governance is the parcellization of authority not on a territorial basis but on the basis of issues. We talk about a humanitarian regime, or a global climate change regime, or about global financial regulation. We cannot elect representatives to participate in decisions in these various fora, especially since the boundaries of different issues tend to change. Governments appoint representatives to take decisions in these different issue areas and these are legitimate since they are appointed by elected governments. What participation of global civil society does is to provide an alternative vehicle for deliberation, for introducing normative concerns, for raising the interests of the individual and not just the state. Global civil society does not represent the 'people'. NGOs, says Michael Edwards, have a voice not a vote.[57] But the fact that global civil society is in principle voluntary and open to all individuals offers the possibility of participation and deliberation at global levels.

Of course, we know that global civil society is dominated by northern NGOs often dependent on funding from government donors. But the concept offers a platform for much wider engagement. It provides a method for reclaiming autonomy on particular issues. It is an opening that needs to be seized if ordinary people are to try to influence the events that affect their lives.

All the same, it is an opening that depends on the control of war. Deliberation requires an 'unfrightened mind'. The development of a humanitarian regime, the transformation of states from war-making to law-making, and the readiness of citizens to commit people and resources to prevent humanitarian suffering are the fundamental conditions for participation and deliberation. The ability to debate and air a range of issues that affect people's lives at global, national and local levels depends on a framework of public security.

6
September 11: The Return of the 'Outside'?

Of course, I am small before the great, weak before the powerful, cowardly before the violent, wavering before the aggressive, expendable before It, which is so vast and durable that I sometimes think it is immortal. I don't turn the other cheek to it. I don't shoot with a slingshot; I look, and then I collect my words.

George Konrad, *Anti-Politics*

The central argument of this book is that the reinvention of 'civil society' can only be understood in the context of the global, in contrast to earlier centuries when civil society only had meaning in relation to a territorial state. I have defined civil society as the medium through which social contracts or bargains are negotiated between the individual and the centres of political and economic authority. Civil society is a process of management of society that is 'bottom-up' rather than 'top-down' and that involves the struggle for emancipatory goals. It is about governance based on consent where consent is generated through politics. In a global context, civil society offers a way of understanding the process of globalization in terms of subjective human agency instead of a disembodied deterministic process of 'interconnectedness'.

Different definitions of civil society are associated with the changing form of social contracts and the changing character of political authority as shown in table 6.1. Thus, in the early modern period, as republican states were emerging from the absolutist forms of rule, civil society was viewed as a rule-governed society (*societas civilis*) contrasted with the state of nature and there was no clear distinction between civil society and the state. In the late eighteenth and nineteenth centuries, as demands for civil rights were extended to political participation so civil society became bourgeois society (*Bürgerliche Gesellschaft*); it was understood as distinct from the newly emerging nation-state and included the economic realm. As social movements began to

Table 6.1 The changing definitions of civil society

	17th and 18th centuries	19th century	20th century	21st century?
Form of political authority	Early modern state and states system	Nation-state and Inter-imperial order	Welfare states and blocs	Global governance including multilateral states
Type of rights	Civil	Political	Economic and social	Global extension of rights
Form of legitimate coercion at global level	War	War and imperialism	Total war and Cold War	International law enforcement
Definition of civil society	Co-terminous with the state, contrasted with anarchy or empire	Distinct from state, includes economic realm but not the family	Distinct from state and capital	Transnational autonomous associations and institutions

demand economic and social rights and to target capital as well as the state, so the meaning of civil society was further narrowed. The new meaning of civil society involves a process of campaigning, lobbying and struggling for a new generation of rights, including gender, the environment and peace, at global, national and local levels. Global governance, a framework of overlapping authorities, is being constituted by and is helping to constitute global civil society.

The new meaning of civil society offers expanded possibilities for human emancipation. Up until 1989, the definition of civil society was territorially bounded. War, defined as a clash between states, was an essential element of the social contracts or bargains that were negotiated. So long as civil society was confined in space, this meant the 'continuous intertwining of real civil societies and war, the ultimate expression of relationships of an uncivil kind . . . This explains why throughout the history of civil societies, war has been a sacred obligation; to wage war against members of other territories has been simultaneously a national and civilising task.'[1] Moreover, civil society only existed in part of the world – primarily north-west Europe and North America. It was contrasted both with those areas that lacked political authority and with states which imposed their authority through coercion

and not through negotiation. This gap between civil societies and
the 'uncivil' part of the world was, at least in part, constructed by
the Europeans both in the ways that they described the rest of the
world and through conquest and exploitation. Global civil society,
I argue, is both an answer to war, a way of addressing the problem
of war, and a vehicle for overcoming this gap.

The reinvention of the concept of civil society was linked to the
wave of new social movements that developed in the 1970s and
1980s. These movements operated outside formal party politics
and were concerned with new issues – gender, environment,
peace and human rights. They were harbingers both of more
radical demands for democracy–autonomy, participation, self-
organization – but also growing global consciousness, the sense
of a common humanity. They also made use of the emerging
infrastructure of globalization – air travel and improved information and communications technology.

The language of civil society, which expressed these aspirations,
was reinvented simultaneously in Latin America and Eastern
Europe, in societies struggling against authoritarianism and militarism, although the East European discourse is better known. In both
cases, there was a similar emphasis on human dignity and on 'islands
of engagement'. The intellectuals in both regions understood civil
society as something distinct from the state, even anti-state, a rol-
ling back of the state in everyday life. And they linked this idea with
transnational concerns – opposition to the Cold War and to
National Security doctrines, and the belief that the reinvented
concept of civil society had global relevance. And in both cases,
these ideas expressed a practical reality: the growth of international
legal instruments that could be used to criticize the state (US
Congressional legislation about human rights in the 1970s and the
1975 Helsinki Agreement respectively); and involvement in transnational networks of activists with North America and Western
Europe, which helped to protect these islands of engagement and
through which the concepts were debated, refined and exported.

The revolutions of 1989 expressed a double phenomenon: the
victory of civil society and the end of war between state or blocs.
The concept of civil society was catapulted into the language of
governments and donors, social movements in other parts of the
world, as well as newspapers and the broadcast media. And as the
term was taken up in other contexts, it acquired other meanings.
Indeed, the rediscovery of the history of the concept, the study of

the classical texts produced a new narrative of civil society that obscured much of what was new about the concept.

One version of the concept was what I call the neoliberal version. In the mood of Western triumphalism that followed the 1989 revolutions, Western commentators claimed that what the revolutionaries wanted was what the West already had and that there was nothing new in their ideas. This was a moment when Western donors were promoting a standard set of recipes for the East and South, known as the New Policy Agenda, for introducing markets and democratic elections on the Western model. Civil society was understood as the instrument for implementing this programme: a way of creating the conditions for the spread of capitalism, promoting formal democracy, generating assent for political and economic reform, smoothing the path of 'structural adjustment' through the provision of social safety nets while minimizing the role of the state, and contributing to the construction of a value system based on trust necessary for efficient markets.

As the energies of the 1980s social movements were dissipated, and as older civic organizations like trade unions were eroded by structural change, funds from Western donors increased, so beginning the process whereby the movements became transformed into NGOs. I use the term 'taming' to describe the process whereby the authorities open up access to social movements and even take on some of their demands, and movements become institutionalized and professionalized. Whereas earlier social movements, like labour and anti-colonial movements, were tamed within a national framework, during the 1980s at least some of the social movements were tamed within a global context. So the concept of civil society was increasingly identified with NGOs and a passive understanding of what civil society meant – a roll-back of the state in a neoliberal sense rather than a reconstitution of political authority at global and local levels.

The 1990s also witnessed the revival of nationalist and religious movements. Many of these movements were extremist and anti-democratic, even though they shared some of the characteristics of the new social movements such as transnational networks, symbolic forms of protest, and reliance on the new media. They can be understood as responses to the turbulence associated with economic and political liberalization and the vacuum created by the collapse of earlier emancipatory ideologies like socialism or

post-colonialism, capitalizing on widespread insecurities and restricting civil society activities. They often have the capacity,
which the more civic-minded groups lack, to reach out to a
broader mass of people who are excluded from the world of travel
and global communication.

The postmodern understanding of civil society arose, at least in
part, as a response to the argument that civil society is culturally
specific, a product of north-west European and North American
society. It is argued that the concept of civil society needs to
incorporate ideas about pluralist communalism to be found in
other parts of the world so as to adapt itself to other cultural
contexts. Civil society is understood as an arena of competing
narratives including those of the groups considered 'uncivil' in
the West; thus the modernist concept of civil society typified
in the West should be viewed as one narrative among many.

What I call the activist version, the version that was developed
in Latin America and Eastern Europe, also continued to be
expressed. Many advocacy NGOs joined together with movements and other groups in civic networks to campaign on particular issues like debt or humanitarian intervention or land mines.
Towards the end of the 1980s, a new movement developed,
which I have called the anti-capitalist movement, similar in form
to the civic networks but broader in its transformatory goals.

I have argued that all these different groups and organizations
need to be considered part of actually existing civil society. The
concept of civil society has a normative content and, in normative
terms, my interpretation is closest to the activist version; civil
society thus consists of those groups and organizations through
which individuals can influence and put pressure on the centres of
political and economic authority, in particular through which they
negotiate new social contracts or bargains at a global level. In
normative terms, non-voluntary communitarian groups should
be excluded since the individual is not free to participate, but in
practice the distinction between the civil and the 'uncivil' between voluntary and compulsory organizations is often difficult
to make. Likewise, passive NGOs primarily concerned with service provision should also be excluded because they do not engage
in public debate, but in practice it is often difficult to distinguish
between service provision and advocacy. Moreover, the neoliberal
version of the concept, despite its shortcomings, has legitimized
the term and provided a conceptual platform on which civic

activists as well as nationalist and religious groups can gain access to the centres of power.

The other side of the coin of the victory of civil society in the 1989 revolutions was the end of war between states and blocs. The post-1989 era created an opportunity to construct a system of global governance, a framework of global rules to manage the process of globalization, composed of international organizations and states organized in overlapping ways and parcelled up according to issues rather than territories. States remain important in this framework as the juridical repository of sovereignty but their character is transformed from being unilateral war-making states into multilateral law-making states. Whether this opportunity will be realized, I argue, depends to a large extent on whether it is possible to create a global security system based on international law which could underpin the framework of global governance. Three forms of warfare were prevalent in the 1990s – network warfare, conducted by networks of state and non-state actors, neo-modern and spectacle warfare conducted by those states that continue to pursue unilateralist policies. There is a real danger that the new types of warfare will overwhelm global civil society. These new types of warfare cannot be contained by territorial borders; the world is no longer divided into zones of war and zones of peace. Nor do these new types of warfare end decisively. On the contrary, they generate extremist ideologies, fear and hate on which such ideologies thrive, as well as a global criminalized economy with a vested interest in extremism.

Pressure from the civic networks of global civil society was particularly important in the humanitarian field during the 1990s and led to a series of important innovations including the notion of humanitarian intervention, understood not as warfare but as policing or international law enforcement, and the International Criminal Court. But it is very difficult to find a single case of humanitarian intervention that can be considered unequivocally successful. Despite the emergence of multilateral states in Europe and some other places, generally associated with a high density of global civil society activities, the commitment to a humanitarian regime has been insufficient both in terms of resources and in terms of readiness to risk lives. Central to the further development of civil society, indeed the preservation of the gains achieved so far, is a new bargain negotiated with the array of global and national authorities responsible for security about global law enforcement and about upholding humanitarian norms.

It is sometimes argued that the concept of global civil society undermines and bypasses democracy since global civil society is self-selecting. 'Who elected the NGOs?' goes the argument. It is true that traditional representative democracy is undermined by the process of globalization, of which global civil society is a part, since so many decisions which affect people's lives are no longer taken by the state alone but in a range of local, regional and global fora. The site of politics has shifted from formal national institutions to new local and cross-border spaces and this is, to a large extent, the consequence of global civil society activities. Apathy at national levels, in part, explains the electoral successes of chauvinist and fundamentalist movements. It is not possible, however, to breathe new life into traditional representative democracy through unilateralism, or a reversal of globalization, nor is it feasible to reconstitute this type of democracy at global levels. Global civil society does provide a way to supplement traditional democracy. It is a medium through which individuals can, in principle, participate in global public debates; it offers the possibility for the voices of the victims of globalization to be heard if not the votes. And it creates new fora for deliberation on the complex issues of the contemporary world, in which the various parties to the discussion do not only represent state interest.

The implications of September 11

So what are the implications of this argument of what happened on September 11 and its aftermath? On one reading, these events mark a significant reversal in the development of global civil society. Both Islamic fundamentalism and the use of terror are profoundly inimicable to global civil society; indeed the attacks on September 11 can be understood as an attack on the basic assumptions of global civility. At the same time, it can be argued, the global unilateralism of the United States, as expressed not only through the war on terror but also the repudiation of treaties like global climate change or the international criminal court, and interference in the functioning of international institutions, undermines both the concrete achievements of global civil society as well as its norms and values; it marks a return to geopolitics and the language of realism and national interest. Above all, the global polarization which results both from terror and the war on terror squeezes the space for global civil society.

Will we look back on the last decade as the 'happy nineties'?[2] Was it an interregnum between global conflicts when utopian ideas like global civil society, human rights, a global rule of law, or global social justice seemed possible?

Or was it, on another interpretation, the moment when global civil society came of age? Was it a moment when the activist understanding of global civil society came into its own, when those who understood civil society not as something the West has and the rest has to learn but as a struggle involving global political change came together to press for an end to violence?

Politicians from multilateral states, as well as independent commentators like George Soros, argued that September 11 exposed the vulnerability of all states and demonstrated the reality of global interdependence. September 11, they claim, represented an opportunity to humanize and civilize globalization, to construct a new set of global rules. On this argument, global civil society is more needed than ever, however discordant and however conflictual, to help set the new global agenda, to reach out across borders to the excluded groups in the world, especially among the Islamic community, to influence popular opinion and so develop a political alternative to fundamentalisms of all varieties.

It is not possible to answer these questions. But it is possible to think about them, to discuss and debate a process which, in itself, is part of the answer. What happened on September 11 was a 'crime against humanity'. There have been similar crimes during the 1990s, in Srebrenica, when 8,000 men and boys were massacred, or in Rwanda, where between 800,000 and a million Tutsis were slaughtered. There have also been large-scale terrorist attacks – the Lockerbie disaster, for example, or the attacks on the American embassies in Kenya and Tanzania. What was unprecedented was the global resonance of the events of September 11. This was above all a global media happening – experienced by millions because the attacks were instantly broadcast, amplified and commented upon. It was a global media happening both because of the reach of contemporary technology and because of the way in which the debates, protests and struggles over global issues over the last decade gave meaning, albeit varied meaning, to September 11.

Al-Qaeda is an extreme example of the kind of fundamentalist movement described in chapter 4. The suicide bombers left no messages; no organization claimed responsibility. But from what we know about network war, it is possible to speculate about the motives. The goal of al-Qaeda is political, to win power in Saudi Arabia and more generally to create an exclusive Muslim Caliphate in the Middle East. In 1998, the organization established the 'World Islamic *Jihad* Against the Jews and Crusaders' and issued a *fatwa* (a ruling to kill) against Americans and their allies. Militants are also asked 'to plunder their money'.[3] The attacks on the Twin Towers and the Pentagon can be understood as a form of political mobilization; the aim was to sow fear and insecurity, to create an environment favourable to the kind of extremist ideology formulated by al-Qaeda. The spectacular character of the attack dramatically raised the public profile of the organization, necessary, as for all such networks, for recruitment and funding.

The response of the Bush Administration was spectacle war. And this perhaps was exactly the response the perpetrators hoped for because it reinforced the sense of fear and insecurity worldwide. This response has to be understood in terms of the political culture of the United States and especially of the Bush Administration. Essentially the attacks on September 11 legitimized a new global unilateralism and military activism, a reversion to the reflexes of the centralized war-making state, a way of renewing governmental support when earlier national bargains were breaking down. It was not a remaking of the bargain because all that American citizens were asked to do was to watch television. They did not have to risk their lives – only two Americans were killed by enemy fire in Afghanistan and twelve by friendly fire. Their taxes were actually reduced. Rather this was a form of populist mobilization that narrows the possibility for the use of public reason, a kind of 'geopolitical soap opera', as Richard Falk has put it, 'pitting good against evil' and generating a 'patriotic fever'.[4]

The end of the Cold War had represented a profound challenge to the way government and society is organized in the United States. For fifty years, the United States was organized on a more or less permanent war footing, which was intimately linked to political, economic and cultural developments. Among the defence and security advisers of President Bush are people who gained their formative experiences during the last years of the Cold War and who have been engaged in an intense debate about how to develop a new military role for the United States after the end of the Cold War and to apply the new Revolution in Military Affairs.

During the 1990s, great efforts were expended in 'imagining' new 'worst-case scenarios' and new post-Soviet threats. With the collapse of the Soviet military-industrial complex, US strategists came up with all sorts of inventive new ways in which America might be attacked, through spreading viruses, poisoning water systems, causing the collapse of the banking system, disrupting air traffic control or power transmission. Of particular importance has been the idea of state-sponsored terrorism and the notion of 'rogue states' that sponsor terrorism and acquire long-range missiles as well as weapons of mass destruction. These new threats emanating from a collapsing Russia or from Islamic fundamentalism are known as 'asymmetric' threats as weaker states or groups develop weapons of mass destruction or other horrific techniques to attack US vulnerabilities to compensate for conventional inferiority.[5] Although the planners never actually came up with a scenario like September 11, the term 'war on terrorism' was already circulating widely. Hence what happened on September 11, and the subsequent anthrax scare, seemed like a confirmation of these anticipations of horror.

Thus for the Bush Administration, the attacks on New York and Washington appeared to be an opportunity to return to the black-white model of the Cold War era, to redraw the boundary between 'inside' and 'outside', to identify a new 'other'. What the Bush Administration tried to do was to impose a war model on what happened reminiscent of the Second World War and the Cold War. First of all the language of the Bush Administration was the language of war and of territorially bound states. The parallel with Pearl Harbour was drawn immediately. Because the enemy had to be a state, Afghanistan was identified as the state harbouring al-Qaeda. But other rogue states, especially Iraq, have been identified, at the time of writing, as targets. American military action was justified as self-defence. The polarizing rhetoric of the war against terrorism magnifies the perceived power and reach of the terrorists; it gives them the respectable status of an enemy, it vests them with the role of an alternative pole to the United States. It narrows the space for dissent, for those who oppose the terrorists and yet remain critical of American policy. 'You are either with us or against us,' said Bush.

Secondly, the global coalition constructed by the US Administration in the aftermath of September 11 was an alliance of states on the Cold War model. It was not, despite the claims of some of the allies, a multilateralist alliance, based on international principles. As in the Cold War period, the criterion for membership in the alliance is support for America, not democracy or respect for human rights. Indeed, the 'war on terrorism' has provided a framework for states, both democratic and authoritarian, to introduce repressive legislation, allowing, for example, the detention for unspecified periods of suspected terrorists. It has also legitimized many 'dirty' wars in the name of the war against terrorism – Israel's heavy-handed actions in the West Bank and Gaza; Russia's war in Chechnya; China's repression against Turkic-speaking Muslims; the Indo-Pakistan conflict; the repression of Muslims in Malaysia, Uzbekistan or the Philippines, not to mention crackdowns on asylum-seekers in Australia and elsewhere. Thus the American approach appears to have given a green light to these local wars on terror, amplifying local cleavages that are reproduced at a global level.

Thirdly, and perhaps most importantly, the military form of the response was 'spectacle war'. The air strikes on Afghanistan were relatively precise[6] and they were effective, in that they created the conditions for the fall of the Taliban and the capture of many al-Qaeda operatives, although not the leadership. They were also widely celebrated in the United States especially as an American victory. But it is not possible to avoid mistakes or so-called 'collateral damage' or even casualties as a result of 'friendly fire'. The number of direct and indirect (as a consequence of the worsened humanitarian crisis) Afghan civilian casualties is greater than the casualties on September 11, as are the numbers of military casualties. Nor is it possible to control what happens on the ground from the air. In the long term, the failure to capture more of the al-Qaeda leadership and to secure a stable environment on the ground may well lead to a reassessment of the Afghan victory.

As in other wars, the consequence both of terror and the war on terror has been to strengthen the position of the unilateralists on all sides. In the USA as well as in other countries, unilateralism is not just a government policy: it commands widespread public support. When the air strikes began on 7 October, 87 per cent of Americans supported them and the same number continued to do so in January 2002.[7] Air strikes against Iraq also appear to have bipartisan support.[8] The same pattern is repeated in the local 'wars on terror'. Thus in Israel, nearly 86 per cent backed the military actions on the West Bank,[9] and in India threatening language against Pakistan is fuelled by a Hindu nationalist base in civil society and in the media. At the same time, the 'Arab Street' is strongly opposed to American action and the majority of Muslim opinion did not believe that Osama Bin Laden was responsible for the attacks of September 11.[10] For many young Arabs in the Middle East, Osama Bin Laden has been transformed into hero and his picture is paraded on demonstrations. The general sense of insecurity seems to have contributed to the success of exclusivist parties in many places, as, for example, the rise of the anti-immigrant right in Western Europe.

In contrast to the Bush Administration, the multilateralist states took the position that the attacks on New York were an expression of global interdependence. The British Prime Minister, Tony Blair, was the most outspoken proponent of this viewpoint. 'One illusion has been shattered on 11 September,' he said, on one of his many speeches on the issue, 'that we can have the good life of the West irrespective of the state of the rest of the world... the dragon's teeth are planted in the fertile soil of wrongs unrighted, of disputes left to fester for years, of failed states, of poverty and deprivation'.[11] Thus the multilateral states have been pushing for greater attention to be paid to global redistribution. France put forward the proposal for a Tobin tax at the Monterrey Financing for Development Summit, while the United Kingdom and the Scandinavian countries pushed for both a substantial increase in and untying of development aid.[12] They have also insisted on the continued importance of international treaties, particularly the International Criminal Court.

But by and large the multilateral states have supported the 'war on terror', arguing, wrongly, that the global coalition is a form of multilateralism. There have been some differences of emphasis. They favoured stabilization for Afghanistan. They have criticized Israeli policies and many countries are warning against the extension of the war to Iraq. But they have not proposed a serious alternative approach. They have not seriously pushed for or tried to implement a law enforcement approach, which might have put more emphasis on stabilization in Afghanistan, for example, or on the introduction of international peacekeeping troops in Israel, something that the UN Secretary-General has courageously demanded.

After the outpouring of sympathy, the civil society reaction to September 11 was initially low-key. The anti-capitalist movement postponed or cancelled many activities. But by 2002, the anti-capitalist movement had began to mobilize again and it was joined by a new and vociferous peace movement which included the veterans of the 1980s peace movements as well as Islamic groups. Thousands of activists took part in parallel summits during 2002, in part stimulated by the new interests in global redistribution of the multilateral states. After the bombing of Afghanistan began, anti-war demonstrations took place throughout the world, including Australia, Brazil, Denmark, Egypt, England, Germany, Greece, India, Indonesia, Italy, Japan, Kenya, Lebanon, New Zealand, Pakistan, South Korea, Spain, Sweden, Turkey and the United States.[13] And, at the time of writing, opposition to a war in Iraq is growing in many countries.

The main thrust of these activities has been opposition to the war on terror; they have, by and large, followed the tradition of anti-military humanitarianism as outlined in chapter 5. A joint statement instigated by the international alliance of civil society organizations Civicus, and signed by thirty-three influential international and national groups, issued on September 21, indicated what was to become the dominant position of these groups; it stated that 'we feel strongly that there is no purely military solution to the kinds of acts that we saw last week. Indeed, the blunt instrument of war may further intensify a cycle of violence and attract new recruits to terror.'[14] Although some groups have talked about international law enforcement, there have been few concrete proposals as to how to deal with network war, of which the al-Qaeda attacks were a classic example. The human rights groups appear to have been sidelined. Human rights groups, both national and international, have done important work in monitoring the new anti-terrorist legislation and documenting how they violate international legal norms. They have also strongly criticized the military tribunals at Guantanamo Bay. They have booked some victories in softening the new laws, for instance in India, and even softening some of the worst features of the military tribunals.[15] But human rights groups have been divided over the war on terror and have not been able to formulate a strong position on international law enforcement as an alternative form of security. As Michael Ignatieff suggested in an article in the *New York Times*, the human rights movement 'will have to engage soon in the battle of ideas: it has to challenge directly the claim that national security trumps human rights. The argument to make is that human rights are the best guarantor of national security.'[16]

One of the more hopeful developments has been the construction of an Israel–Palestine civil society partnership, which criticizes both terror, the suicide bombers, and the war on terror, Israeli occupation. And similar networks can be found among Indians and Pakistanis both in South Asia and among the Diaspora. But as yet, these peace-oriented groups play a marginal role in their societies and as long as the violence continues, there is little space for them to work.

For all these reasons, it is possible to marginalize civil society activities and to dub the majority of the anti-war activists as apologists for terrorism, just as was the case for the anti-Cold War peace movement before links were made with East European opposition groups. Indeed, in so far as the movement criticizes the war on terror without addressing the problem of terror or of network war, they can also be viewed as unilateralist, as the mirror image of the Bush Administration.

Thus the problem is that neither the multilateral states nor global civil society is offering a serious way out of the current impasse. The multilateralists tend to support the war on terror; the peace and anti-capitalist movements oppose it. There is no strong constituency for an international law enforcement position. It is very difficult to imagine a return to the global politics of the 1990s without a stronger effort from the multilateralist states to oppose spectacle war and actually engage in the kind of interventions that would give rise to a greater sense of security and provide the space for alternatives to extremist ideologies on all sides, which are the source of terrorism. Likewise, global civil society has to reach out to civil society in the unilateralist states, in areas where fundamentalism is dominant, and so offer a real alternative to terrorism. It also has to ally with international organizations or their representatives, like Kofi Annan, and press both the unilateralist and multilateral states to take a different stance.

An answer to war?

Spectacle war and network war feed off each other and sustain themselves through fear and insecurity. There is no victory in these types of war, merely destruction. Or rather victory for the

perpetrators is their continued capacity to mobilize political support, not the defeat of the enemy. The attacks on September 11
demonstrated the fact that, in our world of manufactured risk,
you do not need sophisticated technology to inflict mass destruction. The attacks were equivalent to a small nuclear weapon. The
genie of mass destruction has been let loose.

The answer to this destructive stalemate is to minimize violence
at a global level, through the extension of global rules based on
consent. Such an answer is utopian but it may be that only a
utopian answer can offer a way out of this cycle of destruction.
It is often argued that the case for spectacle war rests on the need
to eliminate terror, that, in such a dangerous situation, it is a
luxury to quibble about means. But precisely because it is
no longer possible to achieve a decisive victory, means are no
longer different from ends. As Ken Booth and Tim Dunne put it:
'Rather than letting terrorism win, by allowing fear to be sovereign, terrorism can be defeated today (if not eradicated) by
employing the means, however imperfectly that are the
moral equivalent of the ends we seek...These means-as-ends
would represent a daily victory over terror.'[17]

How can global civil society offer an answer to war? What
are the concrete steps to be taken in order to minimize
violence at a global level? What follows is a set of proposals,
an agenda for debate and discussion – a set of issues that need
to be raised by civil society groups at global, national and local
levels.

First of all, international humanitarian law needs to be strengthened; of special importance is the International Criminal Court.
Moreover international law needs to be applied impartially. It
cannot apply to Afghanistan, Iraq and Serbia and not to Israel,
Russia or China. And the United States cannot exempt itself from
the rules.

Secondly, a substantial multilateral capacity for international
law enforcement needs to be constructed. What is needed is
professional service, which would include both civilian and military personnel, ranging from robust peacekeeping troops, through
police and gendarmerie, administrators, accountants, human
rights monitors and aid workers. The aim of such a service is to
protect civilians before, during and after conflicts, as I spelled out
in chapter 5. Europeans would probably have to bear the brunt of
such a capacity, which should be conceived on an ambitious scale

– a transformation in the structure, training, equipment and deployment of existing military forces – and a massive increased commitment of resources as well as a readiness to risk lives in the service of humanity. The kind of commitment shown in Bosnia Herzegovina or Kosovo needs to be able to be reproduced globally.

Thirdly, there must be intensified efforts to resolve local 'wars on terror' (Middle East, Kashmir, or Chechnya) through:

- The impartial application of international law. Human rights violations and violations of humanitarian law should be condemned on all sides; neither in Israel nor in Russia, for example, does terror justify the kind of tactics adopted by regular forces.
- Support for democrats and moderates who offer an alternative to the extremist ideologies, which characterize both network war and neo-modern militarism. Even if there are only individuals, they need moral and material support. Talks between the 'sides' may be necessary to obtain ceasefires and even agreements but they must be complemented by support for democrats on the ground.
- Readiness to guarantee security and law enforcement, through a sufficient commitment of resources.

Fourthly, in cases where leaders are illegitimate or criminal, which is often the case in conflict zones, as for Saddam Hussein or the Taliban, it is important to find ways to bring about change through support for local political constituencies. External pressure, such as sanctions, especially selective sanctions like freezing bank accounts and refusing visas for the ruling circles, or diplomatic isolation, must pass the test of whether they are thought useful by the local political constituencies. In such cases, as also for local 'wars on terror', the solution is nearly always regional. The support of Pakistan, and indeed Iran, was critical to change the situation in Afghanistan. In retrospect, American military power seems to have been very effective in toppling the Taliban. But given the speed with which the Taliban fell, it could be argued that the same result might have been achieved, albeit more slowly, through ratcheting up external pressure, especially from neighbours; such a result would not have had the same negative long-term consequences as the 'spectacle war'. Likewise, the key to toppling Saddam Hussein is support from Iraq's neighbours. In particular a solution to the Palestinian question would be the most effective way to undermine the political support Saddam Hussein is still able to mobilize throughout the Middle East.

Fifthly there has to be a commitment to global social justice. Poverty and inequality, environmental irresponsibility or the spread of diseases like AIDs/HIV are not the cause of violence. The Middle East, the Balkans and the Caucasus, for example, exhibit relatively high human development indicators – health and education – compared with low-income countries in Africa or Central America. But the continued existence of high levels of poverty and inequality in our globalized world are an argument for and an incentive to violence. The criminalized informal global economy, in which the various extremist networks are often embedded, thrive on unemployment and homelessness. Such a commitment requires resources; there has to be a readiness to pay global taxes or to raise global aid levels. Whether for international law enforcement or for global social justice, not to mention other sorts of global public goods, the budgets of global institutions have to be increased.

Essentially, these five issues could represent the possible content of a global social contract or bargain in which global security is provided through upholding human rights and humanitarian law in exchange for readiness to commit resources through global taxation or other forms of financial transfers and a readiness to risk lives, although not in an unlimited way, in the service of humanity.

Civil society groups who favour such a bargain have to construct alliances with like-minded groups to strengthen their position in the bargaining process with political institutions, companies and other civil society groups of a different persuasion. Such an alliance against global terror and the war on terror would need to include a range of different groups; Israeli peace groups who oppose the occupation of Palestine; Palestinians who oppose suicide bombers; Kashmiri human rights groups who include both Muslims and Hindus; American 'cosmopolitan patriots', as Richard Falk calls them, who dare to challenge the 'geopolitical soap opera'; Europeans who campaign for greater commitments from their governments. Such an alliance can offer a self-reinforcing momentum. American cosmopolitan patriots need to provide active help to Islamic groups who oppose terror, to demonstrate their integrity, to show that their opposition to the war on terror does not mean that they tolerate terror, that it is possible to be critical without being a traitor. In the same way, groups and individuals struggling in difficult circumstances, especially in the Middle East, desperately need outside support but not if it can be dubbed as enemy support.

Above all, it is the job of civil society groups to promote international norms and values, to show that the notion of human consciousness can be actively practised. Michael Ignatieff, in an eloquent essay on human rights, points out that we favour the idea of human equality and dignity not because it is natural.[18] Indeed, the Holocaust, or the attack on the World Trade Towers, demonstrate the opposite; that it is natural to be indifferent to others. The point about concepts like human rights or global civil society is that they are ways of overcoming this natural indifference; they are born of historical experience, of fear, rather than of anything innate. They are the consequence of what Kant called the *asocial sociability* of human beings (see chapter 2). That is why we need civil society alliances, debate, arguments and struggles, why we need a global bargaining process. We need to persuade Muslims, attracted to fundamentalism, that Jews and Crusaders are human beings. And we need to persuade Americans that Afghan or Iraqi lives are equal to American lives.

I am not sanguine that anything resembling this answer will be adopted, although I hope it will be debated. At the time of writing, the prospects are grim. This is probably the most dangerous moment in the lifetimes of those who were born after the Second World War, or perhaps after the Cuban missile crisis. The Bush Administration, with the help of al-Qaeda, has tried to reinvent the 'other' and to revive the 'outside'. But, in the context of global interconnectedness the consequence is likely to be a perverse boomerang effect. As I explained in chapter 4, the boomerang effect is the term used to describe how civil society can use international law, foreign states or international networks to improve their own situation, to bring the 'inside' of human rights and democracy home. The perverse boomerang effect is when military action aimed at suppressing, say, a terrorist network, stimulates further terror instead. The perverse boomerang effect will bring the 'outside' of war and terror home. The 'outside' is likely to be ever present in our societies, a source of insecurity and fundamentalism and of restrictions on freedom. Spectacle warfare, neo-modern warfare and network warfare are engaged in a form of mutual reinforcement. This is the contemporary version of George Konrad's 'It', which I quote at the beginning of this chapter.

In response, global civil society has to 'collect its words'. In this fractured, violent, risky and uncertain world, deliberation offers the best hope for something better. In the aftermath of the Cold War we escaped the threat of total annihilation and liberated ourselves from the hold of a stifling ideological conflict. Now we face a new pervasive transnational set of insecurities. Can we expect more than a conversation or perhaps many conversations? A conversation that is, at least in some degree, 'civilized', that is to say, free of fear, superstition and prejudice. A conversation in which we talk about our moral concerns, our passions, as well as thinking through the best way to solve problems. A conversation in which the participants are not just those who can travel and communicate across long distances, but also ordinary men, women and children. The widespread celebration of the concept of civil society after 1989, even if it was understood very differently in different contexts, allows us space in which to hold such conversations and to create some new 'islands of engagement'. And, perhaps, there is a chance that, as was the case in 1989, these 'islands' can lead to change.

Notes

Chapter 1   Five Meanings of Global Civil Society

1   John Keane, *Civil Society: Old Images, New Visions* (Polity, Cambridge, 1998).
2   John L. Comaroff and Jean Comaroff (eds), *Civil Society and the Political Imagination in Africa: Critical Perspectives* (University of Chicago Press, Chicago, 1999), p. 4.
3   Anthony Giddens, *Runaway World: How Globalisation is Reshaping our Lives* (Profile, London, 1999); and Ulrich Beck, *World Risk Society* (Polity, Cambridge, 1999).
4   Václav Havel, 'The Power of the Powerless', in John Keane (ed.), *The Power of the Powerless: Citizens against the State in Central-Eastern Europe* (Hutchinson, London, 1985).
5   Jean Cohen and Andrew Arato, *Civil Society and Political Theory* (Verso, London, 1992).
6   Margaret Keck and Kathryn Sikkink, *Activists Beyond Borders: Advocacy Networks in International Politics* (Cornell University Press, Ithaca, NY, 1998).
7   See Ian Clark, *Globalisation and International Relations Theory* (Oxford University Press, Oxford, 1999).
8   Chris Brown, 'Cosmopolitanism, World Citizenship and Global Civil Society', *Critical Review of International Social and Political Philosophy*, 3 (2000).
9   Saskia Sassen, *Globalisation and its Discontents* (New Press, New York, 1998).
10   Brown, 'Cosmopolitanism'; David Rieff, 'The False Dawn of Civil Society', *Nation*, 22 Feb. 1999.

11 See ch. 2.
12 This version of global civil society is exemplified in John Keane's essay 'Global Civil Society?', in Helmut Anheier, Marlies Glasius and Mary Kaldor (eds), *Global Civil Society 2001* (Oxford University Press, Oxford, 2001). The term 'globalization from below' is sometimes used in a narrower sense to refer to global social movements, NGOs and networks. See Mario Piantia, *Globalizzazione dal Basso: Economia Mondiale e Movimenti Sociali* (Manifestolibri, Rome, 2001).
13 Rieff, 'The False Dawn'.
14 Keane, 'Global Civil Society?'.
15 Chris Hann and Elizabeth Dunn (eds), *Civil Society: Challenging Western Models* (Routledge, London and New York, 1996), pp. 1 and 4.
16 Brown, 'Cosmopolitanism'.
17 Thomas Dietz, 'International Ethics and European Integration: Federal State or Network Horizon?', *Alternatives*, 22 (1997).
18 Neera Chandhoke, 'The Limits of Global Civil Society', in Marlies Glasius, Mary Kaldor and Helmut Anheier (eds), *Global Civil Society 2002* (Oxford University Press, Oxford, 2002).

Chapter 2   The Discourse of Civil Society

1 *Leviathan*, ch. xiii.
2 Adam Ferguson, *Essay on the History of Civil Society*, (first published 1767; Cambridge University Press, Cambridge, 1995), p. 8.
3 John Keane, *Democracy and Civil Society* (Verso, London, 1988), pp. 31–68.
4 See Anthony Black, 'Concepts of Civil Society in Pre-modern Europe', in Sudipta Kaviraj and Sunil Khilnani, *Civil Society: History and Possibilities* (Cambridge University Press, Cambridge, 2001).
5 See Anthony Giddens, *The Consequences of Modernity* (Polity, Cambridge, 1990).
6 For a discussion of 'civility' see John Keane, *Reflections on Violence* (Verso, London, 1996).
7 Norbert Elias, *The Civilising Process: State Formation and Civilisation* (Blackwell, Oxford, 1982; originally published in German in 1939).
8 According to Adam Smith, 'when law has established order and security, and subsistence ceases to be precarious, the curiosity of mankind is increased, and their fears diminished'; Emma Rothschild, *Economic Sentiments: Adam Smith, Condorcet and the Enlightenment* (Harvard University Press, Cambridge, Mass., 2001), p. 12.

9   Quoted in Robert A. Goldwin, 'John Locke', in Leo Strauss and Joseph Cropsey (eds), *History of Political Philosophy*, 3rd edn (University of Chicago Press, Chicago and London, 1987), p. 507.

10   Tilly prefers national state to nation-state because it is generally assumed that a nation-state involves a homogeneous cultural nation. See Charles Tilly, *Coercion, Capital and European States AD 990–1992* (Blackwell, Oxford, 1992).

11   G. W. F. Hegel, *The Philosophy of Right* (1820), tr. S. W. Dyde, originally published in English in 1896 (Prometheus Books, London, 1996), pp. 185–6.

12   Quoted in John L. Comarolf and Jean Comarolf (eds), *Civil Society and the Political Imagination in Africa: Critical Perspectives* (University of Chicago Press, Chicago, 1999), p. 3.

13   Quoted in Jean Cohen and Andrew Arato, *Civil Society and Political Theory* (Verso, London, 1992), p. 104.

14   Ibid., p. 107.

15   'Americans of all ages, all conditions, and all dispositions constantly form associations. They have not only commercial and manufacturing companies, in which all take part, but associations of a thousand other kinds, religious, moral, serious, futile, general or restricted, enormous or diminutive. The Americans make associations to give entertainment, to found seminaries, to build inns, to construct churches, to diffuse books, to send missionaries to the antipodes; in this manner, they found hospitals, prisons and schools. If it is proposed to inculcate some truth or to foster some feeling by the encouragement of a great example, they form a society. Whenever at the head of some new undertaking you see the government in France or a man of rank in England, in the United States, you will be sure to find an association' (Alexis de Tocqueville, *Democracy in America*, first published 1835 (Vintage Books, New York, 1945), p. 114).

16   Ibid., pp. 117–18.

17   Quoted in Noberto Bobbio, 'Gramsci and the Concept of Civil Society', in John Keane (ed.), *Civil Society and the State: New European Perspectives* (Verso, London, 1988), p. 78.

18   Ibid., p. 82.

19   Quoted in John Ehrenberg, *Civil Society: The Critical History of an Idea* (New York University Press, New York and London, 1999), p. 209.

20   Quoted in Ehrenberg, *Civil Society*, pp. 222–3.

21   See Nancy L. Rosenblum, 'Feminist Perspectives on Civil Society and Government', in Nancy L. Rosenblum and Robert C. Post (eds), *Civil Society and Government* (Princeton University Press, Princeton, 2002).

22 According to Jeffrey Alexander: 'Civil society...should not be equated with trust in an actual government.... To trust faithfully in an actual government, indeed, would be to abandon universalism for the particularism of a party or a state. Civil Society... means trust in universalistic values that abstract from any particular society and that provide critical leverage to particular historical actors.... In strong civil societies, then, distrust of authoritative action and political conflict are omnipresent' (quoted in Andreas Hess, 'The Politics of Civil Society', *Soundings: A Journal of Politics and Culture*, 16 (Autumn 2000)).

23 See Francis Fukuyama, *Trust* (Free Press, New York, 1995); Robert Putnam, *Making Democracy Work: Civic Traditions in Modern Italy* (Princeton University Press, Princeton, 1993).

24 According to Plato, the unity of society is threatened when 'the words "mine" and "not mine", "another's" and "not another's" are not applied to the same things throughout the community. The best ordered state will be the one in which the largest number of persons use these terms in the same sense, and which accordingly most nearly resembles a single person. When one of us hurts his finger, the whole extent of these bodily connections which are gathered up in the soul and unified by its ruling elements is made aware of it and all share as a whole in the pain of the suffering part; hence we say that the man has a pain in his finger. The same thing is true of the pain or pleasure felt when any other person suffers or is relieved' (quoted in Ehrenberg, *Civil Society*, p. 6).

25 Adam B. Seligman, *The Idea of Civil Society* (Princeton University Press, Princeton, 1992), p. 33.

26 Feminist writers argue that the social contract represented a new form of patriarchy in which brothers replaced fathers and the domination of women was legitimized through marriage instead of heredity. See Carol Pateman, 'The Fraternal Social Contract', in Keane, *Civil Society and the State*.

27 According to Hugo Grotius: 'Just as even God, then, cannot cause that two times two should not make four, so He cannot cause that which is intrinsically evil be not evil'. Quoted in ibid., p. 21.

28 See Meghnad Desai, *Marx's Revenge: The Resurgence of Capitalism and the Death of Statist Socialism* (Verso, London, 2002), ch. 2.

29 Adam Ferguson, *An Essay on the History of Civil Society* (Cambridge University Press, Cambridge, 1995 repr. 1999), pp. 13–14.

30 Ibid., p. 24.

31 Ferguson deplores the tendency to assume that 'rude' nations were characterized by vice and misery and his descriptions of the way of life of American Indians are full of admiration for their talents and abilities as well as for their capacity for friendship and

affection. 'Who would from mere conjecture, suppose, that the naked savage would be a coxcomb or a gamester? That he would be proud and vain without the distinction of title and fortune? And his principal care would be to adorn his person and to find an amusement? Even if it could be supposed that he would thus share in our vices, and in the midst of the forest, vie with the follies which are practised in the town; yet no one would be so bold as to affirm, that he would likewise, in any instance, excel us in talents and virtues; that he would have a penetration, a force of imagination and elocution, an ardour of mind, an affection and courage, which the arts, the discipline and the policy of few nations would be able to improve. Yet these particulars are a part in the description which is delivered by those who have had the opportunity of seeing mankind in their rudest condition' (ibid., p. 76). Ferguson himself was a highlander and was nostalgic for the values of the Highlands, which he felt had been lost in commercial society.

32 Ibid., p. 251.
33 Kant, 'What is Enlightenment?', in Kant, *Political Writings*, ed. Hans Reiss and tr. H. B. Nisbet; 2nd enlarged edn (Cambridge University Press, Cambridge, 1992), p. 54.
34 Ibid., p. 55.
35 'Idea for a Universal History with a Cosmopolitan Purpose' (originally published in 1784), in Kant, *Political Writings*, p. 44.
36 Ibid., p. 45.
37 Quoted in Cohen and Arato, *Civil Society*, p. 93.
38 Ernest Gellner, *The Conditions of Liberty: Civil Society and its Rivals* (Hamish Hamilton, London, 1994).
39 Ellen Meiksins Wood, 'The Uses and Abuses of Civil Society', *Socialist Register* (1990).
40 Gellner, *Conditions of Liberty*.
41 Ibid., p. 80.
42 Ferguson, *Essay*, p. 252.
43 Quoted in Marvin Zetterbaum, 'Alexis de Tocqueville', in Strauss and Cropsey, *History of Political Philosophy*, p. 765.
44 See Sunil Khilnani, 'The Development of Civil Society', in Kaviraj and Khilnani, *Civil Society*.
45 Rothschild, *Economic Sentiments*, p. 233–4.
46 Ibid., p. 245.
47 Ibid., p. 252.
48 Cohen and Arato, *Civil Society*, p. 22–3.
49 Ibid., p. xi.
50 Ronnie Lipschutz describes Westphalia as a 'coup from below'. See 'Reconstructing World Politics: The Emergence of Global Civil Society', *Millennium*, 21, 3 (Winter 1992).

51 Ian Clark, *Globalisation and International Relations Theory* (Oxford University Press, Oxford, 1999).
52 Quoted ibid., p. 15.
53 Elias, *The Civilising Process*, p. 104.
54 Tilly, *Coercion, Capital and European States*.
55 Ibid., p. 19.
56 Ibid., pp. 101–2.
57 V. D. Hanson, *The Western Way of War: Infantry Battle in Classical Greece* (Knopf, New York, 1989).
58 Ferguson, *Essay*, p. 193.
59 'In Europe, where mercenary and disciplined armies are everywhere formed, and ready to traverse the earth, where, like a flood pent up by slender banks, they are only restrained by political forms or a temporary balance of power; if the sluices should break, what inundations may we expect to behold? The Romans with inferior arts of communication both by sea and land, maintained their domination in a considerable part of Europe, Asia and Africa over fierce and intractable nations: What may not the fleets and armies of Europe, with the access they have by commerce to every part of the world, and the facility of their conveyance, effect, if that ruinous maxim should prevail, That the grandeur of a nation is to be estimated from the extent of its territory; or That the interest of any particular people consists of reducing its neighbours to servitude' (ibid., p. 148).
60 Ibid., p. 143.
61 De Tocqueville, *Democracy in America*, p. 283.
62 Hegel, *Philosophy of Right*, p. 331.
63 Ibid., pp. 334–5.
64 Pierre Hassner, 'George W. F. Hegel', in Strauss and Cropsey, *History of Political Philosophy*, p. 754.
65 Ibid., p. 758.
66 Jürgen Habermas, 'Kant's Idea of Perpetual Peace: At Two Hundred Years' Historical Remove', in Jürgen Habermas, *The Inclusion of the Other: Studies in Political Theory*, ed. Ciaran Cronin and Pablo de Greiff (MIT Press, Cambridge, Mass., 1998), p. 196.
67 See Daniele Archibugi, 'Models of International Organisations in Perpetual Peace', *Review of International Studies*, 18, 4 (1992), pp. 295–317.
68 Kant, 'Idea for a Universal History with a Cosmopolitan Purpose', p. 47.
69 Jean-Jacques Rousseau, 'Abstract and Judgement of Saint-Pierre's Project for Perpetual Peace' (1756), in Stanley Hoffman and David

P. Fidler, *Rousseau on International Relations* (Oxford University Press, Oxford, 1991).

70 According to Erasmus: 'There are those who go to war for no other reason than that it is a way of confirming tyranny over their subjects. For in times of peace, the authority of the council, the dignity of the magistrates, and the force of law stand in the way to a certain extent of the prince's doing just what he likes!' ('Dulce bellum in expertis', 'Translations from the Adages: From the 1515 Edition', in Margaret Mann Phillips, *The Adages of Erasmus: A Study with Translations* (Cambridge University Press, Cambridge, 1964), p. 349).

71 Kant, *'Idea for a Universal History with a Cosmopolitan Purpose'*, p. 48.

72 Habermas, 'Kant's Idea', p. 176.

73 Ibid., p. 178.

74 Gellner, *Conditions of Liberty*, p. 102.

75 Ibid., p. 22.

76 Ibid., p. 18.

77 Ibid., p. 22.

78 Ibid., p. 23.

79 Ibid., p. 4.

80 Ibid., p. 41.

81 Mahmood Mamdani, *Citizen and Subject: Contemporary Africa and the Legacy of Late Colonialism* (Princeton University Press, Princeton, 1996).

82 Ibid., p. 8.

83 Ibid., p. 289.

84 Partha Chatterjee, 'On Civil and Political Society in Post-colonial Democracies', in Kaviraj and Khilnani, *Civil Society*, p. 172.

85 See Massoud Kamali, 'Civil Society and Islam', *Journal of Sociology* (forthcoming); also Bryan Turner, *Islam and Weber* (Routledge and Kegan Paul, London, 1974).

86 See Farhad Kazemi, 'Perspectives on Islam and Civil Society', in Rosenblum and Post, *Civil Society*.

87 Quoted in Sami Zubaida, 'Civil Society: Community and Democracy in the Middle East', in Kaviraj and Khilnani, *Civil Society*, p. 238.

88 Ali Paya, paper given at Expert Seminar, Meaning and Value of the Concept of Civil Society in Different Cultural Contexts, LSE, 28–9 Sept. 2001.

89 Gellner, *Conditions of Liberty*, p. 5.

90 Cohen and Arato, *Civil Society*, p. ix.

91 John Keane, *Civil Society: Old Images, New Visions* (Polity, Cambridge, 1998), p. 6.

92 T. H. Marshall, *Class, Citizenship and Social Development* (Doubleday, New York, 1964).

93   'The commitment to the purposes of the state', writes Nigel Harris,
      'had to override not only economic calculation of the individual's
      advantage but also the moralities taught in home, school or place of
      worship. The security of the state required its officers and, on
      occasion, its citizens, to lie, cheat, torture or kill, to find guilty
      without trial or even elementary enquiry and to execute. Little
      wonder that those who demurred and embraced pacifism were
      treated not as people with a different opinion but – like homosex-
      uals in the recent past – as creatures of such moral disgust, guilty of
      the unspeakable, no argument was possible, only outraged rejec-
      tion' (*The Return of Cosmopolitan Capital: Globalisation, the State
      and War* (forthcoming)).

Chapter 3   The Ideas of 1989

1   Quoted in Ralf Dahrendorf, *Reflections on the Revolution in Europe*
     (Times Books, New York, 1990), p. 23.
2   Garton Ash, *We the People* (first published Granta Books, London,
     1990; repr. Penguin, Harmondsworth, 1999), p. 154.
3   Quoted in Fred Halliday, *Revolution and World Politics: The Rise and
     Fall of the Sixth Great Power* (Macmillan, London, 1999), p. 53.
4   See Krishan Kumar, *1989: Revolutionary Ideas and Ideals* (Univer-
     sity of Minnesota Press, Mineapolis, 2001), p. 240.
5   Even in the case of the 'how', it can be argued that the ideas were
     not entirely new; the 1989 revolutionaries were able to draw
     inspiration from Gandhian struggles and from Martin Luther King.
6   Václav Havel, 'An Anatomy of Reticence', *END Journal*, 16/17
     (Summer 1985).
7   'Flesh Ties', *New Statesman*, 23 Feb. 1990.
8   Quoted in R. J. Crampton, *Eastern Europe in the Twentieth Century*
     (Routledge, London, 1994), p. 341.
9   Jacek Kuroń, 'Overcoming Totalitarianism', in Vladimir Tismaneau
     (ed.), *The Revolutions of 1989* (Routledge, London and New York,
     1999), p. 200.
10   George Konrad, *Anti-Politics: An Essay* (Harcourt Brace Jovanovich,
     New York and London, 1984) (written in Hungarian in 1982),
     p. 133.
11   Milan Šimecka, 'From Class Obsessions to Dialogue: Détente and
     the Changing Political Culture of Eastern Europe', in Mary Kaldor,
     Gerard Holden and Richard Falk (eds), *The New Détente: Rethinking
     East–West Relations* (United Nations University, Verso, London,
     1989), p. 363.
12   'The Rebirth of Civil Society', Ideas of 1989 Lecture Series, LSE,
     Nov. 1999.

13 Adam Michnik, 'The New Evolutionism', in *Letters from Prison and Other Essays*, tr. Maya Latynski (California University Press, Berkeley, 1985).
14 He himself says that he was not the first to use the term. It was the Czech dissident Jan Tesar in his article 'Totalitarian Dictatorships as a Phenomenon of the Twentieth Century and the Possibilities for Overcoming Them', written in the 1970s and published in 1981 in the *International Journal of Politics*, 11, 1, pp. 85–100.
15 Konrad, *Anti-Politics*.
16 Václav Havel, 'The Power of the Powerless', in John Keane (ed.), *The Power of the Powerless: Citizens against the State in Central-Eastern Europe* (Hutchinson, London, 1985).
17 Milan Kusý, 'The As If Game', in Keane, *The Power of the Powerless*.
18 Quoted in Jeffrey C. Isaac, 'The Meanings of 1989', in Tismaneau, *The Revolutions of 1989*, p. 138.
19 Quoted ibid., p. 138.
20 Quoted ibid., p. 139.
21 Konrad, *Anti-Politics*, p. 231.
22 Havel, 'The Power of the Powerless', pp. 90–1.
23 Konrad, *Anti-Politics*, p. 2.
24 Ibid., p. 92.
25 Ibid., p. 142. Konrad adds: 'We East Europeans have less freedom than Westerners and hunger for it all the more. For that reason, perhaps, we would like to go further than they have in securing individual and collective liberties. If our aim is only to catch up with Westerners in the matter of freedom, as we have tried to do in technology, then of course, we will never catch up with them at all' (p. 184).
26 Ibid., p. 185.
27 Ibid., p. 215.
28 Ibid., p. 211.
29 See e.g. Mary Kaldor and Dan Smith (eds), *Disarming Europe* (Merlin Press, London, 1982), esp. the chapters by Anders Boserup and Dan Smith.
30 Independent Commission on Disarmament and Security Issues, *Common Security: A Blueprint for Survival* (Simon and Schuster, New York, 1982).
31 Milan Kundera, 'The Tragedy of Central Europe', *New York Review of Books*, 19 July 1984.
32 *END Bulletin of Work in Progress*, 1 (1980).
33 Giangiacomo Migone, 'The Nature of Bipolarity: An Argument against the Status Quo', in Mary Kaldor and Richard Falk, *Dealignment: A New Foreign Policy Perspective* (United Nations University, Blackwell, Oxford, 1987).

34 E. P. Thompson, 'Notes on Exterminism, the Last Stage of Civilisation', in E. P. Thompson et al., *Exterminism and Cold War* (Verso, London, 1982).

35 Migone, 'The Nature of Bipolarity'.

36 Konrad, *Anti-Politics*, p. 12.

37 Mient Jan Faber and Mary Kaldor, 'Ending the Occupation of Europe: The Only Way to Save Détente', Paper for the 1984 European Nuclear Disarmament Convention; interview with Medvedev in *END Bulletin of Work in Progress*, 1 (1980).

38 Adam Michnik, 'On Détente: An Interview', in Kaldor, Holden and Falk, *The New Détente*, p. 128.

39 One of the most prominent members of the group who participated in many East–West peace gatherings was Viktor Orban, who became the Hungarian Prime Minister.

40 Quoted in Isaac, 'The Meanings of 1989', pp. 141–2.

41 Ibid., p. 139.

42 Quoted in John Sandford, *The Sword and the Ploughshare: Autonomous Peace Initiatives in East Germany* (Merlin Press/European Nuclear Disarmament, London, 1983).

43 'I Do Have the Right to Make my Voice Heard', *END Journal*, 3 (April–May 1983).

44 *The Spying Game*, BBC 2, 10 Oct. 1999.

45 See Tair Tairov, 'From New Thinking to a Civic Peace', in Mary Kaldor (ed.), *Europe from Below* (Verso, London, 1991); also Alexei Pankin, 'Soviet New Thinking', Ideas of 1989 Lecture Series, LSE, Nov. 1999.

46 This idea was formulated by and can be found in Martin Palouš's writings. See e.g. 'Beyond Politics: Sixteen Exercises in Political Thought', Habilitationsschrift, Charles University, Prague, 1999.

47 Kaldor, *Europe from Below*.

48 E. P. Thompson, *Beyond the Cold War: Not the Dimbleby Lecture* (European Nuclear Disarmament, Merlin Press, London, 1982), pp. 32–4.

49 Charles Tilly, *Coercion, Capital and European States AD 990–1992* (Blackwell, Oxford, 1992), p. 4.

50 Mary Kaldor, 'European Institutions, Nation-States and Nationalism', in Daniele Archibugi and David Held, *Cosmopolitan Democracy: An Agenda for a New World Order* (Polity, Cambridge, 1995).

51 Claus Offe suggests that this is the explanation for the peaceful nature of the revolutions. See Jon Elsler, Claus Offe and Ulrich Preuss, *Institutional Design in Post-Communist Countries: Rebuilding the Ship at Sea* (Cambridge University Press, Cambridge, 1998), esp. ch. 1.

52 Mary Kaldor, *The Imaginary War: Understanding the East–West Conflict* (Blackwell, Oxford, 1991).

53 See ibid.

54 See ibid., ch. 4.

55 Migone has applied the Gramscian distinction between hegemony and domination to the differing position of the United States and the Soviet Union in relation to their blocs. See Giangiacomo Migone, 'The Decline of the Bipolar System, or A Second Look at the History of the Cold War', in Kaldor, Holden and Falk, *The New Détente*.

56 George Orwell, *1984* (Penguin Books, Harmondsworth, 1983; first published 1948).

57 Ulrich Beck, 'The Cosmopolitan Perspective: Sociology in the Second Age of Modernity', *British Journal of Sociology*, 15, 1 (Jan.–Mar. 2000).

58 Alfred Stepan, *Arguing Comparative Politics* (Oxford University Press, Oxford, 2001), p. 101. Stepan describes how a group of businessmen issued a highly critical manifesto in 1975. One of the signatories told Stepan: 'Once we issued the manifesto, civil society entered right into my office by the window. We received numerous invitations to participate in public forums about Brazil's problems and future with members of the Church, trades unions, intellectuals and students – groups we had almost never worked with before' (ibid., p. 96).

59 Ibid., p. 101.

60 Quoted in Jude Howell and Jenny Pearce, *Civil Society and Development: A Critical Exploration* (Lynne Rienner, Boulder, Colo., 2001), p. 209.

61 'A Cautionary Note on Civil Society', Paper presented at Expert Seminar, Meaning and Value of the Concept of Civil Society in Different Cultural Contexts, LSE, 28–9 Sept. 2001.

62 See Margaret Keck and Kathryn Sikkink, *Activists Beyond Borders: Advocacy Networks in International Politics* (Cornell University Press, Ithaca, NY, 1998).

Chapter 4   Social Movements, NGOs and Networks

1 Zygmunt Bauman, *Globalisation: The Human Consequences* (Polity, Cambridge, 1998), pp. 62–3.

2 Robin Cohen and Shirin M. Rai, *Global Social Movements* (Athlone Press, London and New Brunswick, NJ, 2000); see also Jackie Smith et al. (eds), *Transnational Social Movements and Global Politics* (Syracuse University Press, Syracuse, NY, 1997).

3 Margaret Keck and Kathryn Sikkink, *Activists beyond Borders: Advocacy Networks in International Politics* (Cornell University Press, Ithaca, NY, 1998); see also Ann M. Florini, *The Third Force: The Rise of Transnational Civil Society* (Japan Center for International

Exchange and Carnegie Endowment for International Peace, Tokyo and Washington, 2000).

4 Wolfgang H. Reinicke and Francis Deng, *Critical Choices: The United Nations, Networks, and the Future of Global Governance* (International Development Research Centre, Ottawa, 2000).

5 Sydney Tarrow, *Power in Movements: Social Movements and Contentious Politics*, 2nd edn (Cambridge University Press, Cambridge, 1998), p. 3.

6 Ibid., p. 3.

7 Charles Tilly, *Popular Contention in Great Britain 1758–1834* (Oxford University Press, Oxford, 1995).

8 Ibid., p. 38.

9 Tarrow, *Power in Movements*.

10 Ibid., p. 175.

11 R. B. J. Walker, 'Social Movements/World Politics?', *Millennium: Journal of International Studies*, 23, 3 (1994), p. 677.

12 Alain Touraine, *The Voice and the Eye: An Analysis of Social Movements* (Cambridge University Press, Cambridge, 1981).

13 Alberto Melucci, *Nomads of the Present: Social Movements and Individual Needs in Contemporary Society* (Hutchinson, London, 1988); *Challenging Codes: Collective Action in the Information Age* (Cambridge University Press, Cambridge, 1996).

14 Quoted in Donatella Della Porta and Mario Diani, *Social Movements: An Introduction* (Blackwell, Oxford, 1999), p. 12.

15 See Rajni Kothari et al., *Towards a Liberating Peace* (United Nations University, Tokyo, 1989).

16 Rajni Kothari, *Politics and the People: In Search of a Humane India*, vol. 2 (Ajanta Publications, Delhi, 1989), pp. 429–30.

17 Cohen and Rai, *Global Social Movements*.

18 Alan Fowler, *Striking a Balance: A Guide to Enhancing the Effectiveness of Non-governmental Organisations in International Development* (Earthscan, London, 1997), p. 20.

19 E. A. Brett, 'Voluntary Agencies as Development Organisations: Theorising the Problem of Efficiency and Accountability', *Development and Change*, 24 (1993), pp. 269–303.

20 Leon Gordenker and Thomas E. Weiss (eds), *NGOs, the UN and Global Governance* (Lynne Reinner, Boulder, Colo., 1996), p. 22.

21 Charles Chatfield, 'Inter-governmental and Non-governmental Associations to 1945', in Jackie Smith, Charles Chatfield and Ron Pagnucco (eds), *Transnational Social Movements and Global Politics* (Syracuse University Press, Syracuse, NY, 1997).

22 Thus, for example, the International Bureau of Weights and Measures (1875), the International Council for the Exploration of

the Sea (1902) or the International Meteorological Office (1891) all began as non-governmental institutions. See Steve Charnowitz, 'Two Centuries of Participation: NGOs and International Governance', *Michigan Journal of International Law* (Winter 1997).

23   At the 1907 Peace Conference, Baroness Bertha von Suttner welcomed conference delegates and INGOs to tea and lectures every afternoon. Charnowitz, 'Two Centuries'.

24   Ibid.

25   Martha Alter Chen, 'Engendering World Conferences: The International Women's Movement and the UN', in Gordenker and Weiss, *NGOs, the UN and Global Governance*.

26   Robert O'Brien et al., *Contesting Global Governance: Multilateral Economic Institutions and Global Social Movements* (Cambridge University Press, Cambridge, 2000).

27   Helmut K. Anheier, 'Managing Non-profit Organisations: Towards a New Approach', in *Civil Society Working Papers*, 1, Centre for Civil Society, LSE, London (January 2000).

28   See Helmut Anheier, Marlies Glasius and Mary Kaldor, *Global Civil Society 2001* (Oxford University Press, Oxford, 2001).

29   Ibid.

30   See David Hulme and Michael Edwards, *NGOs, States and Donors: Too Close for Comfort?* (Macmillan in association with Save the Children, Basingstoke, 1997).

31   See Leslie Sklair, *The Transnational Capitalist Class* (Blackwell, Oxford, 2000).

32   Helmut Anheier and Nuno Themudo, 'Organisational Forms in Global Civil Society', in Marlies Glasius, Mary Kaldor and Helmut Anheier (eds), *Global Civil Society 2002* (Oxford University Press, Oxford, 2002).

33   G. D. Wood, 'States without Citizens: The Problem of the Franchise State', in Hulme and Edwards, *NGOs, States and Donors*.

34   S. Arllano-Lopez and J. F. Petras, 'Non-governmental Organisations and Poverty Alleviation in Bolivia', *Development and Change*, 25 (1995), pp. 555–68.

35   For a discussion of this perspective, see David Lewis, *The Management of Non-governmental Development Organisations: An Introduction* (Routledge, London and New York, 2001), p. 32.

36   E. Gymah-Boadi, 'Civil Society in Africa: The Good, the Bad, the Ugly', *civnet.org/journal* (May 1997).

37   Patrick Chabal and Jean-Pascal Daloz, *Africa Works: Disorder as a Political Instrument* (The International African Institute, James Currey and Indiana University Press, Oxford and Bloomington, Ind., 1999), p. 22.

38   Lewis, *Management*, p. 199.
39   Fowler, *Striking a Balance*, p. 30.
40   See Diane Osgood, 'Dig it Up: Global Civil Society's Responses to Plant Biotechnology', in Anheier, Glasius and Kaldor, *Global Civil Society 2001*.
41   Quoted in Alex de Waal, *Famine Crimes: Politics and the Disaster Relief Industry in Africa* (James Currey and Indiana University Press, Oxford and Bloomington, Ind., 1997), p. 83.
42   See Keck and Sikkink, *Activists Beyond Borders*, for an insightful analysis and survey of what they call transnational advocacy networks.
43   Manuel Castells, *The Rise of the Network Society*, vol. 1 of *The Information Age: Economy, Society and Culture* (Blackwell, Oxford, 1998).
44   Keck and Sikkink, *Activists Beyond Borders*.
45   Yasmin Jusu-Sheriff, 'The Women's Movement in Sierra Leone', *Conciliation Resources*, 9 (2000).
46   See e.g. Marlies Glasius, 'Expertise in the Cause of Justice: Global Civil Society Influence on the Statute for an International Criminal Court', in Glasius, Kaldor and Anheier, *Global Civil Society 2002*.
47   Fred Halliday, *Two Hours that Shook the World: September 11, 2001: Causes and Consequences* (Saqi Books, London, 2002), p. 47.
48   See Navid Kermani, 'A Dynamite of the Spirit – Why Nietsche, Not the Koran, is the Dangerous Inspiration of the Suicide Bombers', *Times Literary Supplement*, 29 Mar. 2002.
49   Jude Howell and Jenny Pearce, *Civil Society and Development: A Critical Exploration* (Lynne Rienner, Boulder, Colo., 2001), p. 151.
50   See Meghnad Desai and Yahia Said, 'The New Anti-Capitalist Movement: Money and Global Civil Society', in Anheier, Glasius and Kaldor, *Global Civil Society 2001*.
51   Mario Piantia, 'Box 1.2. World Social Forum in Porto Alegre', in Glasius, Kaldor and Anheier, *Global Civil Society 2002*, p. 7.
52   Roland Munck, 'Labour in the Global', and Sarah Ashwin, 'International Labour Solidarity after the Cold War', in Cohen and Rai, *Global Social Movements*.
53   See Colin Hines, *Localisation: A Global Manifesto* (Earthscan, London, 2000).
54   See Desai and Said, 'The New Anti-Capitalist Movement'.
55   World Bank Group, 'An Open Letter', www.worldbank.org/html/extdr/openletter.htm 17 Aug. 2001.
56   Guy Verhofstadt, 'Open Letter: The Paradox of Anti-Globalisation', in *Open Letter on Globalisation: The Debate* (European Council, Laeken, 2001).
57   Robert Graham and Haig Simonian, 'Jospin Sees France as the Pilot of the G8 Protests', *Financial Times*, 24 July 2001.

58 O'Tuathail, quoted in Roland Bleiker, *Popular Dissent, Human Agency and Global Politics* (Cambridge University Press, Cambridge, 2000), p. 31.
59 See Glasius, Kaldor and Anheier, *Global Civil Society 2002*.
60 James Deane, 'The Other Information Revolution: Media and Empowerment in Developing Countries', ibid.
61 'A Cautionary Note on Civil Society', Paper at Expert Seminar, Meaning and Value of Civil Society in Different Cultural Contexts, LSE, 28–9 Sept. 2001.
62 Della Porta and Diani, *Social Movements*.

Chapter 5 Globalization, the State and War

1 See e.g. Kenneth Anderson, 'The Ottawa Convention Banning Landmines, the Role of International Non-Governmental Organisations and the Idea of International Civil Society', *www.ejil.org/journal/vol* 11/No 1.
2 See e.g. Kenichi Ohmae, *The Borderless World: Power and Strategy in the Interlinked Economy* (Collins, London, 1990); or Thomas Friedman, *The Lexus and the Olive Tree* (Farrar, Straus, Giroux, New York, 2000).
3 Paul Hirst and Grahame Thompson, *Globalization in Question: The International Economy and the Possibilities of Governance* (Polity, Cambridge, 1996).
4 David Held et al., *Global Transformations* (Polity, Cambridge, 1999).
5 Anthony Giddens, *The Conditions for Modernity* (Polity, Cambridge, 1990); *The Runaway World*, BBC Reith Lectures, 1999; David Harvey, *The Conditions of Postmodernity: An Enquiry into the Origins of Cultural Change* (Blackwell, Oxford, 1990).
6 Quoted in Roland Bleiker, *Popular Dissent, Human Agency and Global Politics* (Cambridge University Press, Cambridge, 2000), p. 111.
7 Martin Shaw, *The Global State* (Cambridge University Press, Cambridge, 2000), p. 12.
8 Ibid.
9 Roland Robertson, *Globalisation: Social Theory and Global Culture* (Sage, London, 1992).
10 Shaw, *The Global State*, p. 122.
11 Charles Chatfield, 'Inter-governmental and Non-governmental Associations to 1945', in Jackie Smith, Charles Chatfield and Ron Pagnucco (eds), *Transnational Social Movements and Global Politics* (Syracuse University Press, Syracuse, NY, 1997).
12 Shaw, *The Global State*.

13 Giddens, *Conditions for Modernity*; Ulrich Beck, 'Living your Own Life in a Runaway World: Individualisation, Globalisation and Politics', in Will Hutton and Anthony Giddens (eds), *On the Edge: Living with Global Capitalism* (Jonathan Cape, London, 2000).

14 Sol Picciotto, 'Globalisation, Liberalisation, Regulation', MS.

15 Held et al., *Global Transformations*, ch. 1.

16 See e.g. Robert Jackson, *The Global Covenant: Human Conduct in a World of States* (Oxford University Press, Oxford, 2000); also Paul Hirst, *War and Power in the Twenty First Century: The State, Military Conflict and the International System 1500–2100* (Polity, Cambridge, 2001).

17 Charles Tilly, *Coercion, Capital and European States AD 990–1992* (Blackwell, Oxford, 1992).

18 Anthony Giddens, *A Contemporary Critique of Historical Materialism, vol. 2: The Nation State and Violence* (Polity, Cambridge, 1995).

19 Jackson, *The Global Covenant*, p. 19.

20 See C. Murphy, *International Organizations and International Change: Global Governance since 1850* (Polity, Cambridge, 1994).

21 Shaw, *The Global State*, p. 105.

22 Nigel Harris, *The Return of Cosmopolitan Capital: Globalization, the State and War* (forthcoming).

23 Leon Gordenker and Thomas G. Weiss (eds), *NGOs, the UN and Global Governance* (Lynne Reinner, Boulder, Colo., 1996), p. 24.

24 See Robert O'Brien et al., *Contesting Global Governance: Multilateral Economic Institutions and Global Social Movements* (Cambridge University Press, Cambridge, 2000).

25 Mary Kaldor, *New and Old Wars: Organized Violence in a Global Era* (Polity, Cambridge, 1999).

26 Ibid.

27 The term was first used by Michael Mann in 'The Roots and Contradictions of Modern Militarism', in his *States, War and Capitalism: Studies in Political Sociology* (Blackwell, Oxford, 1988), pp. 166–87.

28 As of the year 2000, American military spending in real terms is equivalent to its spending in 1980, just before the Reagan military build-up. More importantly, what took place during the 1990s was a radical shift in the structure of US military expenditure. Spending on military research and development declined less than overall military spending and has increased faster since 1998. As of 2000, US military R&D spending is 47 per cent higher in real terms than in 1980. Stockholm International Peace Research Institute, *SIPRI*

Yearbook 2001: Armaments, Disarmament and International Security (Oxford University Press, Oxford, 2001).

29 Lawrence Freedman, 'The Revolution in Strategic Affairs', Adelphi Papers 318, International Institute for Strategic Studies, London, 1998, p. 70.

30 See J. Der Derian and M. Shapiro (eds), *International/Intertextual Relations: Postmodern Readings of World Politics* (Lexington Books, Lexington, Mass., 1989).

31 See Carl Connetta, 'Strange Victory: A Critical Appraisal of Operation Enduring Freedom and the Afghanistan War', Project on Defense Alternatives, Research Monograph No. 6, 30 Jan. 2002.

32 Martin Shaw, *Risk-Transfer Militarism, Small Massacres, and the Historic Legitimacy of Wars*, 2002. See www.theglobalsite.ac.uk.

33 See e.g. Caroline Moorehead, *Dunant's Dreams: War, Switzerland and the History of the Red Cross* (HarperCollins, London, 1998).

34 Tim Allen and David Styan, 'A Right to Interfere? Bernard Kouchner and the New Humanitarianism', *Journal of International Development*, 12 (2000), pp. 825–47.

35 Ibid.

36 Groups like Bandaid had helped to stimulate a media-orchestrated response to the famine. But other groups argued that Mengistu was creating the famine deliberately as an instrument of war and that the humanitarians were keeping Mengistu in power. MSF, which took this position, was thrown out of Ethiopia at this time. During this period, the NGOs increasingly began to operate without consent, as had happened earlier in Biafra. Indeed in Ethiopia, a split developed among those NGOs that worked in non-governmental areas and those who cooperated with the government. Only the ICRC was allowed to work openly with both sides, although Save the Children managed to do so informally.

37 Interview with Mark Bowden of Save the Children, 9 March 2001.

38 Allen and Styan, 'A Right to Interfere?', pp. 825–47.

39 Margaret Keck and Kathryn Sikkink, *Activists Beyond Borders: Advocacy Networks in International Politics* (Cornell University Press, Ithaca, NY, 1998).

40 www.hrw.org/reports/2000.

41 Noam Chomsky, *The New Military Humanism: Lessons from Kosovo* (Pluto Press, London, 1999); David Chandler, 'The Road to Military Humanitarianism: How the Human Rights NGOs Shaped a New Humanitarian Agenda', *Human Rights Quarterly* 23, 3 (2001), pp. 678–700.

42 See Brahimi, *Report of the Panel on United Nations Peace Operations* (UN Doc.A/55/305-S/2000/809, 21 August) (United Nations, New York, 2000); International Commission on Intervention and

State Sovereignty, *The Responsibility to Protect* (International Development Research Centre, Ottawa, 2002).

43 Charles Jones, *Global Justice: Defending Cosmopolitanism* (Oxford University Press, Oxford,1999).

44 Robert Cooper, *The Postmodern State and the World Order*, 2nd edn (Demos/Foreign Policy Centre, London, 2000).

45 Ibid., p. 22.

46 Ibid., p. 20.

47 Ibid.

48 Ibid.

49 Ian Clark, *Globalisation and International Relations Theory* (Oxford University Press, Oxford, 1999).

50 Ulrich Beck, 'The World Risk Society Revisited: The Terrorist Threat?', Lecture at LSE, 13 Feb. 2002.

51 Philip Bobbitt, *The Shield of Achilles: War, Peace and the Course of History* (Allen Lane, London, 2002).

52 See Anheier, Glasius and Kaldor, *Global Civil Society 2001*.

53 See Mary Kaldor and Ivan Vejvoda, 'Democratization in Central and East European Countries: An Overview', in Kaldor and Vejvoda, *Democratization in Central and Eastern Europe* (Pinter, London and New York, 1999).

54 Cited in Clark, *Globalization*.

55 Richard Falk and Andrew Strauss, 'Next: A Global Parliament', *International Herald Tribune*, 19 April 2002.

56 James Rosenau, 'Governance and Democracy in a Globalizing World', in Daniele Archibugi, David Held and Martin Kohler, *Reimagining Political Community* (Polity, Cambridge, 1998), p. 41.

57 Michael Edwards, *NGO Rights and Responsibilities: A New Deal for Global Governance* (Foreign Policy Centre, London, July 2000).

Chapter 6   September 11: The Return of the 'Outside'?

Epigraph from George Konrad, *Anti-Politics: An Essay* (Harcourt Brace Jovanovich, New York and London, 1984), p. 243.

1 Jeffrey C. Alexander, 'Contradictions: The Uncivilising Pressures of Time, Space and Function', *Soundings: A Journal of Politics and Culture*, 16 (Autumn 2000), p. 100.

2 This was a term coined by Manuel Castells, Conference in Barcelona, Jan. 2002.

3 See Phil Hirschkorn, Rohan Gunaratna, Ed Blanche and Stefan Leader, 'Blowback', *Jane's Intelligence Review*, 1 Aug. 2001; Fred Halliday, *Two Hours that Shook the World: September 11: Causes and Consequences* (Saqi Books, London, 2002); and Hassan Mneim-

neh and Kanan Makiya, 'Manual for a "Raid" ', *New York Review of Books*, 17 Jan. 2002.

4 Richard Falk, 'Testing Patriotism and Citizenship in the Global Terror War', in Ken Booth and Tim Dunne (eds), *Worlds in Collision: Terror and the Future of World Order* (Palgrave, London, 2002).

5 Lawrence Freedman, 'The Revolution in Strategic Affairs', Adelphi Papers 318, International Institute for Strategic Studies, London, 1998.

6 The ratio of civilian casualties to bombs dropped was much higher than during the Kosovo war, reflecting a lower level of precision. See Carl Connetta, 'Operation Enduring Freedom: Why a Higher Rate of Civilian Bombing Casualties', Project on Defense Alternatives Briefing Report No. 11, 18 Jan. 2002.

7 CBS News 'Poll: United We Stand', 9 Oct. 2001, www.cbsnews. com/stories/2001/10/09/opinion/main314059.shtml; CBS News, 'Poll: Support for War Stays Strong', 23 Jan. 2002, www.cbsnews. com/stories/2002/01/23/ opinion/main325303.shtml.

8 Letter from Democratic Congressmen to President Bush, 2 April 2002.

9 Kafala Tarik, 'Israelis Back Sharon', *BBC News*, 8 April 2002, http://news.bbc.co.uk/hi/english/world/middle_east/ newsid_1916000/1916951.stm.

10 Sarah Left, 'Poll: Majority of Muslims Distrusts U.S.', *Guardian*, 27 Feb. 2002.

11 Quoted in *Human Development Report 2002: Deepening Democracy in a Fragmented World* (Oxford University Press, Oxford, 2002), p. 101.

12 Eileen Ciesla, 'The Tobin Test; Meet the New Trial Balloon for Global Tax Advocates', Guest Column, *National Review Online*, 14 Dec. 2001.

13 'Anti-War Protests from Around the World', www.towsonaction-group.org/antiwar.html.

14 'A Joint Civil Society Statement on the Tragedy in the United States', 21 Sept. 2001, www.civicus.org/main/server_navigation/ skeletons/Civicus_01/framework/inde x2.cfm.

15 See Human Rights Watch, *Opportunism in the Face of Tragedy: Repression in the Name of Anti-Terrorism*, www.hrw.org/cam-paigns/september11/opportunismwatch.htm.

16 Michael Ignatieff, 'Is the Human Rights Era Ending?' *New York Times*, 5 Feb. 2002.

17 Ken Booth and Tim Dunne, 'Worlds in Collision', in Booth and Dunne, *Worlds in Collision*, p. 21.

18 Michael Ignatieff, *Human Rights as Politics and Idolatry* (Princeton University Press, Princeton and London, 2001).

Index